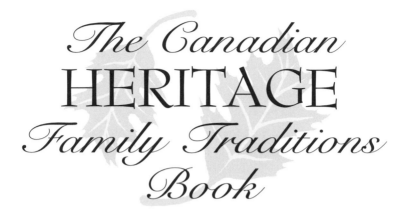

The Canadian HERITAGE Family Traditions Book

Edna McCann

Prentice Hall Canada Inc.
Scarborough, Ontario

Prentice-Hall, Inc., Upper Saddle River, New Jersey
Prentice-Hall International (UK) Limited, London
Prentice-Hall of Australia, Pty. Limited, Sydney
Prentice-Hall Hispanoamericana, S.A., Mexico City
Prentice-Hall of India Private Limited, New Delhi
Prentice-Hall of Japan, Inc., Tokyo
Simon & Schuster Southeast Asia Private Limited, Singapore
Editora Prentice-Hall do Brasil, Ltda., Rio de Janeiro

ISBN 0-13-897604-X

Acquisitions Editor: Jill Lambert
Managing Editor: Robert Harris
Copy Editor: Kelli Howey
Production Editor: Mary Ann McCutcheon
Production Coordinator: Julie Preston
Cover Design: Julia Hall
Cover and Interior Artwork: Carole Black
Page Layout: April Haisell

1 2 3 4 5   F   02 01 00 99 98

Printed and bound in Canada

Visit the Prentice Hall Canada Web site! Send us your comments,
browse our catalogues, and more. **www.phcanada.com**

Table of Contents

Introduction

January
New Year's Day
Epiphany
Eastern Orthodox Christmas
Iroquois Midwinter Festival
Pongal
Chinese New Year
Robbie Burns Day
Ramadan

February
Groundhog Day
Muslim New Year
Lent
Quebec Winter Carnival
St. Valentine's Day
Guyanese Republic Day

March
St. David's Day
St. Cassimir's Feast
Girls' and Boys' Days
Holi
International Women's Day
Purim
St. Patrick's Day

Middle Eastern New Year
Baha'i New Year
Festival de la Cabane à Sucre
Greek Independence Day

April
April Fool's Day
Southeast Asian New Year
Sri Lankan New Year
Cambodian New Year
Thai New Year
Easter
Passover
Ridvan

May
May Day
Santa Cruzan Day
Dutch Liberation Day
Santo Cristo
Mother's Day
Pentecost
Wesak
Victoria Day
Bread and Cheese Day

June
National Strawberry Festival
Father's Day
Dano Festival
Canadian International Dragon Boat Festival
St. John's Day
St. Jean Baptiste Day

CONTENTS

HERITAGE FAMILY TRADITIONS

Rosh Hashanah
Yom Kippur

October

Kingsville Migration Festival
Threshermen's Days
Niagara Grape and Wine Festival
Binder Twine Festival
Lunenberg Fisheries Exhibition and Reunion
Sukkot
Thanksgiving Day
Navaratri
Hallowe'en

November

Guy Fawkes Day
Remembrance Day
Divali
Royal Agricultural Winter Fair
La Sainte-Catherine
St. Andrew's Day

December

Advent
Finnish Independence Day
St. Lucia Day
Hanukkah
Wigilia
Christmas
Boxing Day
New Year's Eve

Introduction

My late husband, George, was a proud and patriotic Canadian. In his opinion, there was no finer place on this earth to live than right here in our own country, Canada.

It came as no surprise to him, therefore, to learn that immigrants numbering in the hundreds of thousands each year left their homelands and arrived in Canada to begin new lives.

It is from joining our original Native Indian, English and French cultures together with this large infusion of our many new and diverse cultures that we are developing our own cultural "heritage" to the point that it exists today. It is a heritage of which we can be exceedingly proud and on which we need to keep working, if we are to continue to improve our overall plan for Canada's future generations.

Heritage is defined as a tradition handed down from one's ancestors or the past. Heritage tells who we are, where we are in the world, what matters to us in our lives and what direction the future will likely take. It brings order and a sense of continuity to our lives. Heritage is also constantly changing, as we add to it our new experiences and develop new beliefs.

It is through learning more about each other's heritage that we reduce prejudices that sometimes slip into our minds about other people who are different from ourselves. Finding ways to help celebrate each other's heritage is one way of beginning to understand each other's point of view.

Those of us who have lived in Canada for years have seen our traditions develop and have become a willing and eager part of the celebrations that have grown with them. It is therefore quite easy for us to relate to those traditions, to understand the reasons behind them and to revel in their celebration. The new Canadians, however, have arrived here having already developed their own set of traditions and their own history. We, being far from the source of their traditions, tend to know very little about them and therefore sometimes find them unusual, strange and even a bit frightening. I hope this book will provide a small stepping stone to understanding some of these many and exciting cultural traditions and the celebrations that have become a part of them.

The timing of the many and varied celebrations has always been established by the seasons and how they relate to the requirements of life for the regions. These changes in the seasons have varied in different parts of the world, and celebrations which began in warmer countries can seem to be very out of place in the Canadian climate. We have inherited our calendar, after many changes and modifications over many centuries, from the Romans who invented it in the eighth century B.C.

After seeing the predictable pattern of the waxing and waning of the moon, they made up a calendar using one complete waxing and waning cycle to represent one month.

The number ten, an important number to the Romans, was used to make a ten-month yearly calendar. They chose to ignore the sixty days between the end of December and the first of March, which was the beginning of their calendar year. (Given our climate, we might have chosen to do the same!)

The first four months of their calendar were named after gods and goddesses, while the remaining six were given numerical names. A later Roman ruler added January, named for Janus, the god with two faces, and February after Februs, the Roman god of purification.

A lunar year has but 354 days. This meant that by the first century B.C., the Roman calendar was about three months ahead of the seasons. Spring festivals were taking place in mid-winter.

In 46 B.C., Julius Caesar corrected the calendar—and that year was 445 days long. To honour this correction, the fifth month was renamed July. August, the sixth month, took its name from Caesar Augustus, the nephew of Julius Caesar. All of the months had thirty or thirty-one days except for February, which had twenty-nine.

One ancient story said that Caesar Augustus was upset that July had thirty-one days, or one more than

August. Thus, he took one day from February to add to his month., leaving February with the twenty-eight days it now has.

This new calendar was based on the "solar year," the number of days it took for the sun to move from its position in the heavens around the earth back to its original position. Caesar realized that each year had about 365 days and 6 hours. Because six hours was a quarter of a day, he decided to add one day every fourth year in order to average out. This fourth year was then called a "leap year."

With scientific advancements, we now know that a year is 365 days, 5 hours, 48 minutes and 49.7 seconds. The Julian and Augustan calendars were too long. For centuries, this minor difference was unnoticeable. But by the sixteenth century the calendar was ten days out.

In 1583, Pope Gregory XIII announced a new calendar to sort out the extra few minutes each year. He calculated that the leap year should be left out three times in every four centuries, during the centenary year, and that this change would make the calendar accurate to one day out of every 3,323 years. A later change made the calendar accurate to only one day out of every 20,000 years!

Catholic countries adopted the Pope's calendar immediately, but others, such as Britain, did not adopt this Gregorian calendar until 1752, and other countries were later still.

Today, this is the official calendar used in most countries of the world, although some still use the lunar calendar for religious affairs. Muslims, members of the Islamic religion, use the lunar calendar, and for this reason, their holidays occur at a slightly different time each year.

The aboriginal people of Canada use a lunar calendar, often adding a thirteenth month during winter to make the days add up properly.

The Jewish calendar is lunisolar, which often needs adjustments. Jewish special days, although not fixed to a specific date (as is Christmas, which is always December 25th), do come in the same season each year because of the adjustments made in the calendar. Hanukkah's dates change each year, yet it is always in December.

Because we here in Canada now have so many cultures, and religions, it would be impossible to touch on every celebration. On the following pages, I hope to give you just a sampling of the rich and varied heritage that is now ours to share.

January - Chinese New Year
Before the Chinese New Year, houses are
swept clean, new clothes are worn
and debts are paid. Quarrels must
be settled so that everyone may have a
new beginning.

February - St. Valentine's Day
February 14th is St. Valentine's Day. A
special day that is special in many countries
around the world, it is enjoyed here in
Canada in a number of different ways.
Cards, flowers, candy and gifts can tell
someone how much you care.

March - St. Patrick's Day
March 17th is the day when those of us
who are of Irish ancestry (and even many
who are not) celebrate St. Patrick's Day, a
day for "wearin' o' the green."

January - Chinese New Year

February - St. Valentine's Day

March - St. Patrick's Day

January

Old One, lie down
Your journey is done,
Little New Year
Will rise with the sun.
Now you have come to
The foot of the hill,
Lay down your bones,
Old Year, and lie still.

Young One, step out,
Your journey's begun.
Weary Old One
Make way for his son.
Now you have started
To climb up the hill,
Put best foot forward,
New Year, with a will.

Eleanor Farjeon

As the chimes strike midnight, we welcome the beginning of a new year. Our celebrations on this day take many forms.

In French Canada, New Year's Day is very much a family celebration. For several years, George, the girls and I enjoyed welcoming the New Year with the Pouliot family in Quebec City. Early in the day, as was the custom, Paul, the Pouliot's son, would ask for the father's blessing before the entire family would head off to the celebration of the New Year's Mass at the nearby Roman Catholic church. Back in those days, after Mass Père Noël would visit, bringing gifts for all of the children. (Today, Père Noël visits on Christmas Eve.)

Later in the day, all of the Pouliot clan would gather at Paul and Madeleine's home for a special dinner. As Paul came from a large family, this meant that about fifty aunts, uncles and cousins would arrive, bringing many *tourtière* meat pies and dried apple pies, traditional specialties. It was a loud and joyous day that was enjoyed by young and old.

For the Greek-Canadians, New Year's Day is called St. Basil's Day. It is a traditional family celebration where gifts are exchanged with family members and friends. As well, each family bakes a *basilopita*, an orange-flavoured sponge cake baked with a coin hidden inside. The person who gets the slice with the hidden coin will have good luck all year. As well, a deep fried bread called a *lalangita* is used by Greek-Canadians to predict luck in the New Year. Made from a simple dough with raisins, it is much like a donut. The first *lalangita* is made in a cross shape, and, if it spins and turns over to the right when dropped into the hot fat, things will go well for the family in the year to come.

For those of the Buddhist faith, this is Temple Day in Canada. Kyomi Ito, a friend of mine who lives in Toronto, tells me that if you are near Ontario Place on New Year's Eve, you may hear the Buddhist welcome to the New Year. At midnight, the Buddhist community tolls a bell 108 times to end the old and ring in the new.

Japanese-Canadians of the Shinto faith welcome the New Year today. Wearing their best clothes, they will visit shrines where they will pray for the renewal of hearts, good health and prosperity.

For the Japanese, the first meal on New Year's Day is *ozoni*. This soup is made with chicken pieces, *dashi*, *daikon* and other vegetables, and each of the vegetables brings a different form of luck to the New Year. *Ozoni* is served in deep bowls over pounded sweet rice cakes.

Macedonian-Canadians will eat a special pastry called a *maznik*. This cake, as with the Greek *basilopita*, contains a coin for good luck. Before serving, the cake is turned three times and then cut into the exact number of pieces to serve the whole family, including pets.

Just a few days later, on January 5th, Macedonian-Canadians, following the old custom of the Julian calendar, light an enormous bonfire on the eve of *Koleda*. The men sit around the bonfire until early morning, when they visit from house to house singing their wishes for a long and healthy life. People in the homes visited serve special food in thanks for the good wishes.

One of the most interesting New Year's Day celebrations here in Canada is the levee held in Victoria, B.C. Some years ago, George and I enjoyed the festivities in this beautiful city with our friends the McNeills. At Government House, we met the Lieutenant-Governor and his wife and enjoyed some sherry and Christmas cake while we explored the historic building. Anyone may attend this reception, and there was quite a large crowd of us hobnobbing with the resident dignitaries. From Government House we moved to City Hall, where we met and chatted with the Mayor. The weather on that day was balmy, even for Victoria, and from City Hall we went to the harbour, where the McNeills' forty-foot sloop awaited. Under the winter sun and pushed by a mild breeze, we spent the rest of the day sailing in the Strait of Juan de Fuca. It was one of my most memorable New Year's Days ever!

Our friends who are of Korean origin celebrate their New Year, called *Solnal*, today. It is a time for the children and adults to wear the traditional *han pok* costumes, which are brightly coloured and beautifully decorated. Children are treated with fruit, gifts and money and the family eats a traditional rice soup called *ttukgook*. The New Year period ends on the day of the first full moon, usually fifteen days after Solnal.

Whatever your origins, food usually plays a special role on New Year's Day. My mother always made a delectable pie that we children called New Year's Pie. It is really quite delicious and perhaps it will become a part of your New Year traditions.

New Year's Pie

1/2 cup finely chopped candied fruit

1/4 cup light rum

1 envelope plain gelatin

1/4 cup cold water

2 cups light cream

1/2 cup sugar

2 eggs, separated

9-inch pie shell, chilled

1. Combine the candied fruit and rum and set aside. Soften the gelatin in the cold water.
2. Combine cream and 1/4 cup of sugar and heat in a double boiler.

3. When hot, add softened gelatin and stir until dissolved.

4. Beat the egg yolks and add the hot cream mixture gradually, stirring constantly.

5. Set over boiling water and stir until thickened.

6. Remove from heat and cool until slightly thickened, stirring frequently.

7. Beat the egg whites until stiff and fold the remaining 1/4 cup of sugar into them.

8. Fold the egg whites into the gelatin mixture.

9. Chill again until nearly ready to set firmly, then fold in the candied fruit mixture and spoon into the chilled pie shell.

10. Chill several hours before serving.

NOTE: Either a pastry or crumb crust may be used.

A delicious way to welcome the New Year!

Over the years, it has been common practice for many of us to make New Year's resolutions to better our lives in the year to come. "I will lose ten pounds," "I will be better organized," "I will spend more time with my family," are often promises made and then broken. It is possible that this tradition may have its origins in several cultures.

Before a Scottish family celebrated *Hogmanay* (the welcoming of the New Year), it was the custom to clean the home, return to the rightful owner anything that was borrowed, pay all debts, mend all clothing and tune all instruments.

Before the Chinese New Year, houses are all swept clean, new clothes are worn and debts are paid. As well, quarrels must be settled so that everyone may have a new beginning.

It seems that all of us look forward to a new beginning, a chance to do better and a happy, healthy New Year.

January 6th is the celebration of Epiphany. In the Western Church, it is the day to commemorate the coming of the Three Wise Men who were led by the Star of Bethlehem to the birthplace of the infant Jesus.

> *And, lo, the star, which they saw in the East, went before them, until it came and stood over where the young child was. When they saw the star, they rejoiced with exceeding great joy. And when they were come into the house, they saw the young child with Mary, his mother, and fell down and worshipped him: and when they had opened their treasures, they presented unto him gifts; gold and frankincense and myrrh.*

Matthew 2: 9–11

On the eve of Epiphany, in Quebec, there is a Twelfth Night celebration. French Canadians, following a tradition dating back to the middle ages in France, make a cake called the *Galette des Rois*. The cake contains a charm or a *fève* (bean), which enables the person who finds it to become "king or queen" of the party.

My granddaughter, Phyllis, once spent "Twelfth Night" with French-Canadian friends in Montreal. She was lucky enough to find the bean in her slice of cake and thus became the "queen." She was then responsible for organizing the activities for the evening. Card games were very popular, but Phyllis also organized a scavenger hunt that was talked about for years after.

This night is also a popular time to go "a-wassailing," or drinking "wassail" to the health of friends and neighbours.

Wassail, wassail, all over town

Our bread it is white and our ale it is brown;

Our bowl it is made of the green maple tree,

In the wassail bowl we'll all drink unto thee.

"Wassail, Wassail"
traditional English song.

My friend, Mary Stewart, sent along two different recipes for "wassail," one traditional and one that would be served to all ages.

Traditional Wassail

2 large green apples

20 whole cloves

2 cups Burgundy wine

2 sticks cinnamon

1/2 cup brown sugar

2 cups apple juice

1/2 tsp. nutmeg

1/2 tsp. ground ginger

two 12-oz. cans (or bottles) ale

(If you choose to omit the ale, change the recipe to one quart of Burgundy and three cups apple juice.)

1. Core the apples but do not peel them. Cut the apples to make thick rings and stud each ring with three or four cloves. Place the apples in a shallow baking pan. Bake in a pre-heated 350° F oven until they are barely tender when pierced with a fork (20 to 30 minutes).

2. Stir the other ingredients together in a kettle. Heat just to boiling, stirring occasionally.
3. Float apples in wassail. Serve warm.

Yield is about 9 cups.

Wassail for All Ages

2 qts. grape juice

1 qt. apple juice

1 pt. lemonade

1/4 cup honey

2 sticks cinnamon

1/2 tsp. whole cloves

1 lemon (cut in 1/4-inch slices), or apples sliced and baked as in traditional wassail.

1. Stir together first six ingredients in a kettle. Heat to boiling, stirring occasionally.
2. Float the fruit slices on top of the hot punch just before serving.

Makes about 14 cups.

When George, the girls and I lived on Canada's East Coast, going "a-wassailing" on Twelfth Night was a very popular tradition in our small village. Many of our neighbours were of British or Scottish ancestry and we enjoyed the open houses in the old tradition. It was also a nice lead-in to the "Feast of Kings" celebrated by our Acadian friends the next day.

Russian-Canadians, Ukrainian-Canadians and other members of the Eastern Orthodox Church celebrate Christmas according to the Julian calendar, on January 7th. On Christmas Eve, there is a family celebration in the Ukrainian home. It usually begins with a holy supper of twelve meatless dishes. (Many members of the Orthodox Church have forty days of partial fasting before Christmas and during this time they do not eat meat or dairy products.)

Olga Babinetz, a friend and neighbour who came to Canada from the Ukraine, was happy to welcome me to her family's celebration just last year.

A lighted candle had been placed in the window to guide travellers. This is in memory of Mary and Joseph's journey. In Saskatchewan, where there are large communities of Ukrainian-Canadians, the lighted candles in the windows are like tiny beacons up and down every street.

The meal began when the children, who were all outdoors, saw the first star in the night sky. They hurried back inside where their father offered an ancient blessing followed by the traditional greeting "Christ is born! Let us glorify Him."

In the corner of the dining room was placed a *didukh*, or sheaf of wheat, to symbolize the gathering of the family.

As we sat down at the table I saw that some hay had been arranged under the tablecloth and on the floor, to represent the manger where Jesus was born.

Olga's son, Jasha, tasted the first of the twelve dishes, the *kutia*, made from boiled wheat mixed with poppy seeds, honey and nuts. Each of us, in turn, then ate a spoonful the *kutia*, which stands for the family unity and prosperity. Chelsey, the family cat, and Herschel, the dog, also shared in the *kutia*.

The rest of our meal was a happy jumble of eating, talking and laughing. We enjoyed borsch, cabbage rolls and dumplings, along with several other vegetable dishes; twelve in all.

After dinner, we gathered 'round the piano to sing old Ukrainian and English Christmas carols. Had we been in a large Ukrainian community, we probably would have gone carolling from house to house.

I headed for home after a delightful evening of good food and family fun, while Olga and her family left to attend the midnight Mass service to welcome Christmas.

For the people of the Iroquois nation, the New Year begins five days after the visit of the first new moon in January. The Midwinter Festival lasts for eight days and is celebrated by wearing traditional clothing, feasting, dancing and participating in games and chanting ceremonies. The ceremonies are often held in the longhouse or the community centre. In years gone by, the Iroquois hunters stocked the longhouse with a large supply of meat for the Midwinter Festival. Meat is still an important part of the feasts today, and boiled beef or venison are popular.

If you are interested in seeing a restoration of the Iroquois village, you need look no further than the Crawford Lake Conservation Area in rural Milton, Ontario, not far from Toronto. Originally discovered in 1972, the settlement has been heralded as one of the most interesting discoveries in Native history. A large portion of the village has been reproduced to exact specifications from its origins (estimated to be between 1434 and 1459).

There are some excellent educational programs for students at Crawford Lake that are informative but good fun as well. My great-granddaughter, Jenny, has made several trips to Crawford Lake and has picked up more fascinating information each time.

Jenny and her friends learned to play a child's version of the sacred Peachstone game, a betting game played by the Iroquois during the last days of the Midwinter Festival.

In the children's version, the peach stones, painted black on one side, are placed in a bowl. The stones are then tossed into the air and caught in the bowl.

The player is awarded one point for every stone that lands coloured-side up. After a predetermined number of tosses, the player with the most points wins.

During the Midwinter Festival, the Iroquois beg the Creator for life and for the continuity of their lives in tune with the rhythms of nature.

> *What is life? It is the flash of a firefly in the night. It is the breath of a buffalo in the winter time. It is the little shadow which runs across the grass and loses itself in the sunset.*
>
> *Crowfoot, Blackfoot chief on his deathbed in 1890*

There are a number of celebrations held in January and *Pongal* (also called *Makara Sankranti*) is just one of the many. It is a three-day harvest festival in India, celebrating a newly-harvested rice which has been ceremonially cooked. In some areas of India the rice is fed to cows and bullocks, whose horns have been painted with bright colours for the festival. In other areas the festival may be celebrated with a bullfight or with dolls, displayed in homes for three days. Because January is no time for harvest here in Canada, Pongal is celebrated by Indian-Canadians as a cultural evening with singing and dancing.

A Jewish celebration that takes place in Israel is also celebrated here in Canada. The Jewish New Year of Trees or *Hamishhah Asar Bishvat* is observed by having trees planted, usually one for each boy and girl. Here in Canada, Jewish families often arrange to buy trees to be planted in their children's names. The Canadian children observe the day by eating fruits that have been imported from the Holy Land.

One of the most colourful celebrations takes place sometime between January 21 and February 20. The Chinese New Year is actually a double celebration. It is a time of hope—and the birthday of every Chinese. Traditionally, a Chinese person is considered to be one year old the day that he or she is born. The following New Year's Day another year is added. It is interesting to see that someone born on New Year's Eve becomes two years old the next day. The Chinese New Year is a family gathering and, by tradition, the most important festival of the year. In China, celebration of the New Year often lasts for an entire month; here in Canada, it usually lasts a little longer than a week.

It is important to see family members and friends face-to-face during this time. This is said to ensure good luck for the future. Because Chinese families prefer the conviviality and closeness of the family gathering, the public celebration of the New Year is usually staged on the weekend.

On New Year's Eve there is a family feast when the old year is bid farewell and the new year is welcomed.

Red is the predominant colour when the banquet table is set for dinner. Tablecloths, napkins and candles are the beautiful and bright "Chinese Red" of the celebration. As in the Ukrainian dinner, there are meatless dishes served—but for the Chinese, it is because no harm may be caused to obtain the food: you may not kill an animal for this dinner.

The twelve vegetarian courses of the dinner represent the twelve-part cycle of years in the Chinese zodiac (these are the Rat, Ox, Tiger, Hare, Dragon, Serpent, Horse, Sheep, Monkey, Rooster, Dog and Boar, in that order).

The dinner is served slowly and there are always leftovers for the next days, when no cooking may be done.

Even the youngest children are encouraged to stay awake long into the night, for it is believed that the longer the children are awake, the longer the parents will live.

"*Gung hay fah choy*," the Chinese greeting for luck and prosperity, or "*Kung hsi fa tsai*," Mandarin for "best wishes for good fortune," are the salutations of the day on Yuan-Tan, New Year's Day.

Visitors to the home are given gifts of sweets and fruits and the children receive red envelopes called *lai-see* that contain money. Children also are given rice cakes and oranges, which signify good wishes for happiness.

On Pender Street, in the heart of Chinatown in Vancouver, B.C., thousands of Chinese and tourists mingle together to enjoy the New Year celebration.

The restaurants serve such delights as abalone, crab, lobster, roast duck and suckling pig. After dinner, the throng returns to the streets that are decorated with lanterns, where the dragon leads the parade of lion dancers and where the "evil spirits" are chased away by exploding fireworks.

Many other Asian groups also celebrate the New Year around this time. Vietnamese, Laotians and Cambodians share many similar customs with the Chinese. For them the New Year is also the most important event of the year, and the family is the focal point of the celebrations.

January 25th is the date of the most celebrated Scottish event in Canada. This is "Burns Night," held to honour the favourite Scottish poet, Robert Burns, born on this day in 1759. All across Canada, in Scottish clubs, in community centres and in private homes, commemorative dinners are served, nearly always beginning with the traditional "haggis."

Several years ago, I was delighted to be invited to the home of Ross and Lucy McLean. Not everyone there was of Scottish background, but you could never have guessed. All the men sported kilts, knee socks, ruffled shirts and velvet jackets. The ladies were also beautifully attired in Scottish garb and ready to participate (if not enjoy) in the haggis. A good friend of the McLeans played the bagpipes and "piped in the haggis" for Ross to carve. It has become quite a ceremonial ritual to pipe in and carve the haggis. During dinner we were each called upon to read a poem or propose a toast to the famous poet. After dinner we danced and enjoyed Scottish music before singing the best-known of all Robbie Burns' works, "Auld Lang Syne." It was a memorable evening, made even more special by my own Scottish heritage.

Celebrated by Muslims around the world, Ramadan is a month of prayer and fasting. Ramadan is the ninth month of the Islamic calendar, and during this month Muslims who are physically able do not eat or drink from dawn to dusk. Because the Islamic calendar is lunar, the time of Ramadan changes each year. Ramadan is a time of worship and contemplation; a time to strengthen family and community ties.

February

February 2nd is celebrated in several ways here in Canada. The most amusing is Groundhog Day. The "weatherman," a groundhog best known as Wiarton Willie, is said to come out of hibernation to see if he can see his shadow. If he sees his shadow, according to those who believe in this prediction, there will be six more weeks of winter. No shadow means spring will come early.

February 2nd is also Candlemas Day. Falling as it does halfway between winter solstice and spring equinox, it too is looked on as a prognosticator.

If Candlemas Day be fair and bright,

Winter will have another flight,

But if it be dark with clouds and rain,

Winter is gone and will not come again.

In its religious form, Candlemas Day is celebrated by blessing the candles for sacred use.

February is designated as "Black History Month" in Canada. Originally it was called Negro History Week when it began in the United States in 1926. The month of February was chosen because it was the birth month of both U.S. president Abraham Lincoln and Frederick Douglass, a Maryland–born mulatto and runaway slave, whose book, *Narrative of the Life of Frederick Douglass*, stirred sympathy in the North for escaped slaves.

Canada played a unique role in American history. Our country was the end of the "underground railway" line, a prearranged route along which runaway slaves could come north to Canada and find freedom. It's estimated that 30,000 black slaves escaped as a result of this underground railway.

I'm on my way to Canada,

That cold and distant land,

The dire effects of slavery

I can no longer stand

Farewell old master,

Don't come after me,

I'm on my way to Canada,

Where coloured men are free.

"The Free Slave"
a song by American abolitionist George W. Clark

Many of the men, women and children who arrived in Canada made their home in Elgin Settlement in North Buxton, near Chatham, Ontario.

Today, the Elgin Settlement is one of the few remaining black Canadian settlements that have been in existence since the pre-Civil War days. Today the settlement is inhabited, for the most part, by descendants of the original settlers who chose to remain in Canada.

My daughter Marg, son-in-law Bruce and I visited the museum in North Buxton that was opened as a memorial to the Elgin Settlement. There was so much to see, as the Raleigh Township Centennial Museum has a well-stocked research library, a cultural room featuring the work of local black artists, and much emphasis placed on the history and accomplishments of the original settlers.

Many organizations across Canada observe Black History Month, including the Black Cultural Centre for Nova Scotia (many blacks settled in "Africaville" in Nova Scotia, having arrived by the underground railway), the Ontario Black History Society and the Black Historical Society of British Columbia.

Presentations and workshops are held at many schools and cultural centres. As well, African-Canadians are encouraged to participate in activities that teach them about their heritage. A call to any of the above organizations will tell you where to go to enjoy performances or exhibits by black artists.

There are a number of religious celebrations in the month of February. For our friends of the Muslim faith, *Eid-Ul-Fitr* marks the end of Ramadan and heralds the Muslim New Year. This day is marked by family gatherings and visits from friends. Usually, gifts are exchanged and delicious foods are enjoyed. One of the traditional dishes is *sawine*, made with milk, raisins, chopped almonds and vermicelli.

Lent, the Christian period of fasting before Easter, often begins in February (although it can start as late as March 8th).

The day before Lent begins is called Shrove Tuesday. Also known as "Pancake Tuesday," the custom of eating pancakes is said to have begun because it was the practice to try to use up the fat and drippings to fry the hot cakes before entering the meatless days of Lent.

Growing up as I did, the daughter of a minister, this time of year had a particular significance for our whole family. My father explained to us that just as Jesus had sacrificed for forty days in the wilderness, so should we honour Him with a sacrifice of our own.

I remember one year, when I was very young, being angry about Lenten expectations placed on me. When Father asked what I would be giving up for the forty days, I announced "peas, lima beans and wearing long underwear" (all of which I hated). Father, in his infinite wisdom, was non-judgmental with his calm reply, "All right, Edna."

Of course, later I was completely ashamed of myself but much too proud to admit it; so rather than say anything, I just gave up a number of things over the next forty days that really were significant to me.

In his sermon on Easter morning, Father mentioned how self-sacrifice, without drawing attention to it, was a sign of maturity, and the true meaning of Christianity. Without him saying so directly, I knew how proud he was of me.

There are also many winter festivals held all across Canada. Given our weather at this time of year, it is hardly surprising that many of the festivals include winter sports.

The Sourdough Rendezvous is the three-day Winter Carnival held in Whitehorse, Yukon Territory. Dog team and snowshoe racing, curling and hockey as well as moose calling contests are highlights. Vernon, B.C., builds a giant ice palace and Queen Silver Star reigns as Queen of the carnival that features ski championships, a pioneer parade, curling and skating, as well as a torchlight parade.

Edmonton, Alberta, hosts the Mukluk Mardi Gras. Named for the traditional Eskimo boot, many of the events are in keeping with the theme. There are snowshoe and dog team races along the Saskatchewan River and a moccasin dance, and a giant igloo made of ice is the site of the ice sculpting contest. In the community of The Pas, Manitoba, the Trappers' Festival celebrates the men who developed the immense fur trade industry. The activities are related to the trappers' lives and include dog team racing, rat skinning, trap setting, ice fishing, tree felling and canoe portaging. Exhibits also include beaded buckskin articles from the Indians and the Métis. The voyageurs are honoured for their place in Canadian history at the Festival du Voyageur in St. Boniface, Manitoba. Their traditional costumes of *capotes* (blanket-cloth coats) and red toques are a highlight of the parade.

The Ottawa winter carnival, now known as "Winterlude," runs for ten days in early February. Dog sled derbies, motorcycle races on a frozen lake, ice sculpting and skating on the Rideau Canal are all part of the fun in our nation's capital.

The Quebec Winter Carnival was originally created in 1894 to break the monotony of the long winter. The present carnival format, with *"Bonhomme Carnival,"* the giant snowman mascot, is held just prior to the beginning of Lent. There is a giant ice palace and an ice sculpting contest that draws contestants from around the world. Thousands of tourists flock to Quebec, where they are treated to such interesting sights as day and night parades, the ice canoe race across the frozen St. Lawrence river from Quebec to Lévis, barrel jumping contests, a dog derby and costume balls.

A highlight of the Quebec Carnival is the International Peewee Hockey Tournament, which now draws hockey teams from as far away as Finland, Sweden and Russia.

Many years ago, the young son of some good friends played in the tournament. Jim McDowell was a goaltender for the Humber Valley Indians and his mother and father, Marion and Neal, accompanied their son to this prestigious event. I talked with Jim about his memories of the games. He spoke with tremendous enthusiasm. "It was fantastic! We had never played with more than twenty-five or thirty fans in the stands and suddenly we were in the *Colisée*, playing against a team from Montreal, and the arena was packed to the rafters. It could have been intimidating, but we played a sensational game and at the end Carl Varga and I were selected as stars of the game—Carl scored and I got a shutout. I'll never forget getting a standing ovation from twelve thousand people! I also recall being interviewed by Charlie Hodge, an N.H.L. goalie, for local television—pretty heady stuff for a twelve-year-old. As well, I remember how wonderful my "family" (the people with whom I was billeted) were. They came to every game and cheered wildly whether we won or lost, as we did before we made it to the finals. It was an absolutely incredible experience and I relive it each February as I see the youngsters who play in each successive tournament."

February 14th is St. Valentine's day. It is a day that is special in many countries around the world and is enjoyed here in Canada in a number of different ways. Cards, flowers, candy and gifts can tell someone how much you care.

St. Valentine's Day honours St. Valentine, a Christian martyr who died in the third century. The celebration associated with St. Valentine probably derived from the ancient Roman Feast of Lupercalia, which was held on February 15th. On that day, it was the custom for young men and maidens to draw partners for the coming year. As the number of Christians increased in the empire, Lupercalia became linked to the feast of St. Valentine held on February 14th. And so, St. Valentine became known as the patron saint of lovers.

One of the nicest Valentine's Days for our family came at a time when George and I had just moved to a new parish. We had three young daughters, little money, and were wondering what to do to celebrate.

A member of our new church arrived at our home with a turkey dinner complete with mashed potatoes, gravy, vegetables and dessert. Candles set in silver candlesticks and a card reading "A Valentine welcome to you all" gave us a Valentine that I have never forgotten.

Not all Valentines are this elaborate, but all are sent with love.

For Canadians who have come from the South American country of Guyana, February 23rd is celebrated as Republic Day. On this day in 1970,

Guyana became the Co-operative Republic of Guyana within the Commonwealth of Nations, and a president, selected by the National Assembly for a six-year term, became the Head of State. Here in Canada, this event is celebrated with a dinner and dance on the Saturday closest to the twenty-third.

I became interested in learning about the Guyanese struggle for independence after I met Nadira Brancier, her husband Mark and their children Mark and Natasha, who all live in Ontario. Nadira's father, Dr. Cheddi Jagan, became the Executive President of Guyana on October 9, 1992, after the country's first free and fair election since independence. He remained President until his death March 6, 1997.

Nadira is justifiably proud of her parents and their contribution to her native land during the long and arduous struggle for independence.

As creator of the People's Progressive Party in 1950, Dr. Jagan's goal was to attain independence for Guyana and to build a democratic and socialist state. He and his wife, Janet, worked tirelessly within the party in the face of discrimination, state violence and corruption.

In the words of Moses Nagamootoo, minister of information at the time of Dr. Jagan's death, "Cheddi Jagan stood out for his honesty in public life and his uncompromising commitment to a vision of a better quality of life for the people of Guyana and the world. He was greatly admired for his incorruptibility."

I'm sure that Guyanese-Canadians appreciate and celebrate the Jagans' contribution to Guyana, and no one will appreciate or understand that legacy better than Nadira Brancier and her family.

March

T he first day of March is St. David's Day for the
Welsh. According to legend, daffodils burst into
bloom on March 1st in honour of this saint. Another
legend suggests that the Welsh won a victory over
their Saxon enemies by having the men wear leeks in
their hats so that they would recognize and then not
kill their own men. Here in Canada, people of Welsh
ancestry wear a leek in their hatband and a daffodil
in their lapel on this day.

I well remember the celebrations on the Sunday
nearest St. David's Day when we were in Alberta.
The church was incredibly beautiful with vases and
pots of daffodils placed on the window ledges, and
the strains of "Men of Harleck," sung in the native
Welsh tongue, would send chills up my spine.

M acedonian and Bulgarian-Canadians follow an
interesting Old World custom on March 1st.
Small tokens, made of red and white thread, are
worn pinned to the lapel. *Marteniki*, as they are
called, used to be small pieces of red and white
thread twisted together. They were thrown for the
storks or swallows to make their nests. Here in
Canada, the *marteniki* are usually offered to the first
robins of spring.

Just a few days later, Lithuanian-Canadians celebrate their patron saint's birth with a banquet. This dinner is called St. Cassimir's Feast and it follows the church service on the Sunday nearest March 4th. Often there is a fundraising bazaar held in connection with the banquet, organized by the Lithuanian Boy Scouts and Girl Guides.

After the long winter, we here in Canada anxiously await the first signs of spring. If you live in the Toronto area, you have an opportunity to enjoy the new season a bit early. On the first weekend in March, the Japanese-Canadian Cultural Centre holds a spring festival where visitors may enjoy a display of ceremonial dolls, Japanese dancing, martial arts and delicious national foods.

The focal point of the celebration is the *Hina-Matsuri*, or the Dolls Festival, traditionally held on March 3rd. Also called Girls' Day, it is the custom to celebrate girls' growth and good health by displaying sets of fifteen or more ceremonial dolls and miniature household items on tiered shelves called *hina-dan*. The *hina-dan* are covered with red cloth and the dolls on display have often been handed down for many generations. Called the *dairi-sama*, and dressed in *heian* period costumes, they represent the Emperor and Empress, their noble court ladies in waiting, ministers and musicians.

Although Boys' Day, *Tango-No-Sekku*, used to be celebrated on May 5th, many Canadian families now choose to celebrate Girls' and Boys' Days together.

In Japan, it is the custom to place tall bamboo poles with cloth or paper streamers shaped like carp in the yard of each home. When the wind blows, it appears that the fish are swimming. The carp, a fish with energy and power, is able to fight its way up fast-moving rivers and waterfalls. Its strength and determination is said to represent a growing boy, and each family flies one carp streamer to represent each son.

In Canada, the family will often celebrate with a meal that includes *hishimochi* (diamond-shaped rice cakes) and by drinking *shirozake* (made with rice malt and sake).

Those members of the Hindu faith have two celebrations to enjoy, one religious and one a spring festival.

Mahashivaratri is celebrated as the Night of the Great Lord Shiva, one of the major deities to whom Hindus direct their devotion.

The night before the feast, four worship ceremonies, or *pujas*, are held. Texts are recited, songs are sung and stories are told before the twenty-four-hour fasting period ends with a great feast.

Holi is one of the most boisterous and exuberant Hindu festivals, during which men, women and children smear each other with coloured powder (*gulal*) and throw coloured water on each other.

The Holi festival is a day when good triumphs over evil, light vanquishes darkness, and the earth gives birth to a brand-new cycle of growth.

Although Holi has roots deep in ancient Hindu mythology, this joyous festival is now celebrated by people of different faiths.

Canadian Hindus celebrate Holi with dancing, singing and feasting.

In Canada, women regard their right to vote and participate in government as a natural part of our democratic system. It was not always so, and in many areas of the world, equality for women is just a dream.

International Women's Day on March 8th is a day set aside for us to express our concerns about the inequality of women's rights worldwide. Although we here in Canada have made significant advancements toward equality, there remain many areas for improvement.

March 8th was chosen because it is the anniversary of the first protest march, held in 1857 in New York City, to protest the appalling working conditions for women in the textile and garment industry.

It's interesting to note how many women are now involved in politics. Not that long ago, women didn't even have the right to vote; now they are installed as members of cabinet. Many women also hold positions of power in major corporations across the country.

As we head toward March 21st and the spring season, I am reminded of a delightful "rite of spring" in the British Columbia city of Victoria. Known for its more temperate climate, springlike temperatures are often enjoyed in Victoria much earlier than in the rest of Canada. One week early in March is declared "Flower Count Week." During this week, men, women and children alike go to their gardens or into gardens in public areas and count the number of flowers that they see. So popular has the Flower Count become that schools now give students an hour off to participate in the tallying of crocuses, daffodils or other spring flowers.

The numbers of flowers counted are phoned in to a special Flower Count Centre, and each day the grand total is announced on the radio and television. A local mall even shows a graph of the count.

For the past several years, our local television station has picked up the coverage of the event. I confess that it is difficult not to feel pangs of jealousy as I see people in shirt sleeves or light jackets strolling in a garden, while I look out the windows to see leftover snow and no visible signs of spring.

These lines from William Wordsworth bring me hope of spring.

It is the first mild day of March,

Each minute sweeter than before.

The redbreast sings from the tall larch

That stands beside her door.

My granddaughter, Phyllis, and her husband Bill have close friends of the Jewish faith. Each year at this time, they and their children, Justin and Jenny, enjoy celebrating the Feast of Lots, known as Purim, with the Rosenbaum family.

The story of Purim is found in the book of Esther. It describes the escape of the Persian Jews from a massacre planned by Haman, prime minister to the King. The massacre was averted when Queen Esther overheard Haman's plans to kill all the Jews in the kingdom. Using a *purim*, a kind of dice, he had cast lots for the date for his plan. With Esther's help, the Jews were well-armed and prepared to defend themselves. The next day they celebrated their victory over Haman.

Purim is a favourite festival among Jewish children. Usually the *Megillah* (the scroll of Esther) is read aloud. Each child has a noisemaker called a *gregger*, and each time that the name "Haman" occurs in the story, the children drown out his name by shaking the *gregger* or by hissing and booing.

A favorite Purim treat is a three-cornered filled pastry called a Hamantaschen. The cookies are said to represent Haman's three cornered hat.

There are many excellent recipes for Hamantaschen cookies, but Phyllis selected this easy one so that the children could make the cookies themselves.

Hamantaschen Cookies

1 stick (4-oz.) unsalted butter, softened

2 tbsp. confectioner's sugar

2 egg yolks

3 tbsp. ice water

1 1/2 cups flour

apricot jam

butter (to grease the pan)

1. Cream the butter and sugar together in a large bowl. Add the egg yolks and continue to mix well.
2. Add the ice water. Gradually stir in the flour until a ball of dough is formed. Place the dough in plastic wrap and refrigerate it overnight.
3. The next day, remove the dough from the refrigerator.
4. Preheat the oven to 350° F.
5. Grease the cookie sheet with butter.
6. Roll out the dough on a clean lightly floured surface to a 1/4-inch thickness. Using the top

of a glass with about a 3-inch diameter, press out the cookies.

7. Place a spoonful of jam in the centre of each circle. Make a three-cornered shape by bringing the three sides together and pinching them.

8. Place the Hamantaschen about an inch apart on the greased cookie sheet and bake until lightly browned along the edges.

Other popular fillings are poppyseed with honey and almonds, prune jam, honey-raisin nuts and prune filling.

March 17th is the day when those of us who are of Irish ancestry (and even many who are not) celebrate St. Patrick's Day, a day for the "wearin' o' the green."

My father was of Irish background and he revelled in the celebrations of this day. He was often seen wearing a bright green tie or sweater for the occasion and he even bought a Kelly green bowler hat that he wore with pride (in spite of the fact that it sent us children into gales of laughter).

Many people assume that the Irish wear green on St. Patrick's Day because Ireland is called the

"Emerald Isle." In fact, the real reason has been nearly forgotten now. Hundreds of years ago, the people of Ireland burned green leaves and boughs in the spring. The ashes were then spread over the fields in the belief that this would make the land richer. Those who wear green on this day are honouring this ancient custom.

One of my father's favourite Irish proverbs is also beloved by me:

> *May the road rise to meet you; may the wind be always at your back, may the sun shine warm upon your face. May the rain fall soft upon your fields and until we meet again, may God hold you in the palm of his hand.*

March 21st brings us the spring equinox, the day when the hours of daylight and darkness are equal.

For Canadians of Middle Eastern extraction, it is the time to celebrate *Now Ruz*, or the New Year. Several days before the festival begins, people participate in an important custom, fire jumping. Bonfires are lit and participants leap over the fires to symbolize their hope of strengthening the sun so that the cold of winter will be conquered and warm spring weather will come again.

Another custom of the Now Ruz celebration is the breaking of an old clay jar. The woman of the house breaks an old clay jar outside the door of the home to symbolize all of the quarrels of the previous year being thrown away.

The Now Ruz festival began more than 2,500 years ago, and was originally a Zoroastrian celebration called *Jamshedi Navroz*. Zoroastrians believe that King Jamashed is the same person that the Christians and Jews call Noah. Jamshedi Navroz is the day that the animals were sent from the ark out into the world after the great flood, to begin anew. This is probably why Jamshedi Navroz is so closely associated with the Now Ruz, celebrated in Iran, Iraq, Afghanistan and other parts of the Middle East.

As well, the Baha'i New Year is also called the Feast of Now Ruz. The feast marks the end of an eighteen-day fast, and the celebrations are similar to those of the Zoroastrian faith.

Haji Firuz, a clown with his face painted black like a mummer, comes out to community gatherings. Here he sings, dances and pokes fun at people like political leaders or business owners. He gives out small gifts of food while collecting money from the crowds who gather to watch his antics.

The celebration of Now Ruz begins at the exact moment that the equinox occurs. Some years this means getting up in the middle of the night.

As many family members as possible join together for the feast. The table is set with symbolic objects, all beginning with the sound "*s*" in the Persian language. Sugar is for sweetness in the New Year, fruit for happiness, sprouted seeds for food and the cultivation of the earth, coins for wealth, flowers to show the earth's productivity, vinegar for preservation and spices to symbolize the spice of our life.

As well, a coloured egg is a symbol of life and the world.

An orange floating in water has particular significance, as it is believed that the orange will tremble at the exact moment that the New Year begins.

Family tables are also set with a candle for each family member, and a mirror because it is considered good luck to see your own face and the faces of others.

After reading from a holy book, such as the Zoroastrian Avesta or the Islamic Koran, it is time to eat sweets and exchange gifts.

As with all New Year's celebrations, it is time to resolve conflicts, share wonderful meals and enjoy the company of family and friends.

Long before the Europeans came to North America, the aboriginal people collected the sap from the sugar maple trees.

An old folktale attributes the accidental discovery of maple syrup to a family squabble. One day, a squaw asked her brave to fill a cooking utensil with water. She placed the pot at the base of a maple tree and returned to her wigwam. The brave, angry at being asked to perform such a menial chore, gouged the tree with his tomahawk and left. The next morning his wife retrieved the pot, and found that it contained enough liquid—which she mistook for water—to cook some venison. She cooked the meat with the syrup, which proved to be delicious, and from that time many of us have come to love maple syrup.

For years, trees were tapped individually and sap was collected in buckets. Children in many areas were given time off school to help with the drilling of holes, collecting of sap, and the boiling down process known as "sugaring off."

The process of sap collecting has been modified in many areas, with plastic hoses joining together to bring the sap to one large holding tank.

Native people in many areas still celebrate with thanksgiving for the spring harvest. Manitoulin and Parry Islands on Lake Huron are still the sites of special ceremonies that include prayers of thanks, good food, craft displays and lots of fun.

In Quebec, the *Festival de la Cabane à Sucre* is still a most popular event. Some years ago, my husband George and I were visiting with friends in *"la Belle Province."* We travelled with them south from Quebec City to the small town of Beauceville. There, we joined a number of other syrup lovers in collecting the sap buckets and stoking the fire in the *cabane à sucre*, or the sap house, to boil down the syrup.

At noon, we enjoyed a wonderful feast of ham, eggs, potatoes, pancakes and French bread, all covered in hot, delicious syrup.

There is a wonderful beauty in the snowy woods and the whole family can enjoy this very Canadian activity.

On Canada's East Coast, sugaring off parties are called *licheries*. When the syrup is just at the point of turning to toffee, children (and candy-loving adults) scoop up the mixture on a big stick and then scrape some off for each person on a little palette. The syrup is licked like candy, but, the East Coast being the East Coast, they eat salt cod and roasted potatoes to take the edge off the sweetness!

On March 25th, Greek-Canadians don their traditional clothing from the early 1800s and celebrate their Independence Day with folk dancing and feasting.

In fact, the day is a double celebration in the Greek community, as it is also Annunciation Day, the old Christian holy day celebrating the archangel Gabriel's announcement to Mary that she would be the mother of Jesus.

It's appropriate, isn't it, that the beginning of life for our Lord should have begun in spring, the time of renewal?

April

The first day of April, some do say,
Is set apart for All Fools' Day.
But why the people call it so,
Not I, nor they themselves do know.
But on this day are people sent,
On purpose for pure merriment.

Poor Robin's Almanac

To many people around the world, April 1st is All Fools' Day, or April Fools' Day. No one knows for sure how it originated, but it was celebrated in France more than 400 years ago. Because the sun is leaving the zodiac sign of Pisces (or "the fish"), the French call it *Poisson d'avril*.

Whatever the origin, it is now the time for sending people on false errands, trying to make them believe impossible stories or generally playing tricks. Some years ago, even the staid B.B.C. joined in the fun. The early morning news announced that Italy had a bumper crop of spaghetti. Goodness knows how many people were actually fooled, but I'll bet that there were a few.

As Mark Twain once said, "The first of April is the day we remember what we are the other 364 days of the year."

On April 2nd, thirteen days after Now Ruz, the Middle Eastern New Year's celebration comes to an end. The day is called *Sizdeh Bedar* and, in warm areas of the world, it is a day to picnic and enjoy the countryside. Because thirteen was considered to be an unlucky number in ancient times, people spent the day away from home, and even now Persian descendants follow this ancient tradition. As well, many people choose to take the seeds that were sprouted in the clay dishes for Now Ruz and spread them in a field or float them down a stream. This was once a good luck ritual for crops, but now it is done with hope for a lucky and happy new year.

Sizdeh Bedar is also a day to play tricks on family and friends, much in the manner of the April Fools.

As children, my brother, my sister and I were given much encouragement to read. My mother and father were avid readers, but it was my father who fostered in us the passion for literature.

George and I tried to do the same with our daughters and they, in turn, have inspired this love in our grandchildren and great-grandchildren.

Now my daughter Marg and I spend many happy hours at our nearby elementary school reading to youngsters whose parents, for whatever reason, have not had much time to read to them. It is so gratifying to see the look of pure joy on the children's faces when they realize that they are able to read all by themselves.

For this reason, April 2nd holds a special place in my heart. It is International Children's Book Day, appropriately set on the birth date of Hans Christian Andersen, the Danish poet and storyteller. The International Board on Books for Children chose this day to celebrate children's books from around the world.

We here in Canada have many outstanding authors of children's books. One of the favourites of the children I read to is Robert Munsch. His stories, although written for youngsters, hold a great appeal for adults as well. I often find myself laughing aloud as I enjoy his tremendous sense of humour and the exaggerations that so appeal to young readers.

Although many festivals celebrate spring as a time of renewal and new life, the Chinese choose this time to remember friends and family members who have died.

Ch'ing Ming, a spring festival, is a day to visit the graves of ancestors. For three days before Ch'ing Ming, no hot food is eaten and no fires may be lit. On the day itself, family members tidy the burial sites, plant flowers and offer gifts of food and wine, clothing and furniture.

In the tradition of the Chinese religion, when a person dies his or her spirit lives on. If the spirits are unhappy, then they will cause trouble for those still living. For this reason, burial sites are carefully chosen and members of the family are buried close to one another.

I find many of the Ch'ing Ming traditions so interesting.

After the gravesites have been cleaned, a meal is eaten at the graveside. Before the meal begins, tea or wine is poured on the ground around the grave to soothe the spirits. As well, a portion of the food from the meal is set aside for the departed souls. After the meal, a ceremony is often held where pieces of paper representing money, clothing and furniture are burned in the hope that the "spirit" of the offerings will reach the dead ancestors.

After this ceremony, many families spend the rest of the day flying kites. When evening comes, candles are placed inside the kites which makes them glow as they twist their wild patterns in the darkening sky.

Japanese-Canadians of the Buddhist faith celebrate *Hana-Matsuri* on April 8th. A flower festival celebrating the birth of Buddha, its likely beginning came from the legend that said that Buddha was born in a lotus flower. A special religious ceremony is held in honour of this occasion.

Although many of us in Canada celebrate the new year in January, our friends from Southeast Asia celebrate their New Year in mid-April. This is because their calendar is based on the movement of the moon and stars as well as the sun, and thus their solar new year is celebrated in mid-April.

There are several celebrations at this time. *Baisakhi*, on April 13th or 14th, is New Year to Hindus, Buddhists, Jains and Sikhs from Sri Lanka, Bangladesh and India. It is especially significant to the Sikhs. In 1699, Guru Gobind Singh initiated his five disciples. After a test of faith, these five men became his Five Beloved or *Panj Piare*. They drank *amrit*, a mixture of water and sugar, from a steel bowl as a symbol of their devotion to their Guru. Since then, Baisakhi has become the traditional day for people to make the decision to follow the Sikh way of life.

Here in Canada, special services are held in the *gurdwaras*, or Sikh Temples. The "five "Ks," symbols of faith, are worn by all dedicated Sikhs. These are *kesh* (uncut hair), *kangha* (comb), *kirpan* (actual or symbolic sword), *kachs* (short trousers worn under outer clothing) and *kara* (steel bracelet worn on the right wrist). Those in the Khalsa Panth, or Brotherhood of the Pure, created by Guru Singh, are given names. Each Khalsa brother is given the name *Singh* (or lion) and each sister *Kaur* (or princess).

On the day after Baisakhi, April 14th, the Sri Lankan community in Ontario celebrates its New Year with a ceremonial meal and a cultural program. Friends and family gather together to exchange gifts, often including betel leaves, and the for the seeking of forgiveness.

Cambodian-Canadians, many who of whom live in the Montreal area, celebrate their New Year, *Bon Chol Chhnam*, with a traditional morning religious program. The Buddhist monk makes his ritual speech and then families partake in a ceremonial meal, eaten in the Eastern style, with fingers.

In the evening, there is often a party where speeches are given and traditional food is enjoyed with much music and dancing.

The Thai New Year, or *Songkran*, is a three-day celebration. In Thailand, this is the hottest time of the year, and Songkran is a water festival involving the throwing of water on one another for good luck, bathing Buddha images, and pouring scented water over the hands of the elderly as a sign of respect.

Here in Canada, as in Thailand, it is customary to clean the home. It is believed that anything old and useless must be thrown out or it will bring bad luck to the owner. Although it is too cold here in April to throw water on one another, Thai people enjoy parties with traditional food and dancing.

For those of us of the Christian faith, the Easter celebration is the basis of our religion—belief in the life to come after death.

Easter Day falls somewhere between March 22 and April 25, but the celebration of Easter actually begins on Palm Sunday, the week before Easter.

Palm Sunday commemorates Christ's triumphal entry into Jerusalem. Two of his disciples met him at the foot of the Mount of Olives and from there Jesus rode into the city while welcoming throngs ran before him shouting *Hosannas* and waving branches of palm trees.

Ride on! Ride on in majesty!

Hark! All the tribes hosanna cry

O, Saviour meek, pursue Thy road

With palms and scattered garments strowed

The Book of Common Prayer

Long ago, the Palm Sunday ceremony was a sort of religious pageant. In the Roman Catholic Church, the entry of Christ into the Holy City was reproduced by a priest riding a donkey, leading a procession back to the church while branches and flowers were scattered before him.

There are many traditions connected to Palm Sunday. Welsh families refer to Palm Sunday as "Flowering Sunday." Family gravesites are tidied up and then decorated with spring flowers to prepare for Easter.

Czechoslovakian children collect bouquets of pussy willows and take them to church where they are blessed by the priest.

In some communities, Palm Sunday is designated "Children's Feast." Children and the clergy make a procession around the church singing Easter hymns. The children carry lighted candles that have been decorated with ribbons and flowers.

Germans give everyone in the family a brown egg (eggs have long symbolized life and regeneration).

In the days prior to Palm Sunday, George and the girls and I spent many hours shaping palm fronds into the shape of a cross. Each of our parishioners was given one of the symbolic crosses at the end of the Palm Sunday service. Some of my friends from the early parish have told me that they have kept their Palm Sunday crosses with them and that they are used as bookmarks in their Bibles or hymnals. I know that the girls are happy to know that their hard work is still appreciated.

The Thursday of the Holy Week, Maundy Thursday, marks the day on which Jesus ate the last supper with his disciples. Often the churches are specially cleaned and the altars are washed. At the supper, Jesus washed the feet of his disciples and it later became the custom of the kings and queens of England to wash the feet of the poor and to give them gifts on this day. "Maundy Money" was presented to as many poor people as there were years in the monarch's age.

Good Friday, the day of Jesus' death by crucifixion, always had special meaning for George and me. There were a great number of services in Holy Week, and the added responsibilities often left him tired. However, the solemnity of the day seemed to give him renewed strength and often his Good Friday service was one of his finest of the year. How proud I was of him as he sang, unaccompanied, The Reproaches.

I can still close my eyes and hear his voice as he read from the Book of Luke:

> *And Jesus crying out with a loud voice said "Father into Thy hands I commit my spirit," and having said this, He breathed his last.*
>
> *Luke 23:46*

It never failed to move me to tears.

Good Friday is also a day to enjoy hot cross buns. Thought to have originated in ancient Greece, these small cakes were offered to the Olympic gods. The buns were tiny loaves of bread, spiced and sweetened and marked with a design shaped like an ox's horns. The early Christian Church copied the custom but changed the design to that of the cross.

This is an old family recipe recipe for Hot Cross Buns.

Hot Cross Buns

1 cup milk, scalded

1/2 cup sugar

3 tbsp. melted butter

3 tsp. salt

1 yeast cake

1/4 cup warm water

1 egg, well beaten

3 cups flour

1/2 tsp. cinnamon

1/2 cup currants

1 tsp. grated lemon peel

1 pinch ground cloves

1 egg, well beaten

confectioner's sugar and milk

1. Combine scalded milk, sugar, butter and salt. When lukewarm, add yeast cake dissolved in the 1/4 cup water.
2. Then add egg and mix well.
3. Sift flour and cinnamon together and stir into the yeast mixture. Add currants, lemon peel and cloves. Mix thoroughly.
4. Cover and let rise in a warm place until double in size. Shape dough into round buns and place on a well-buttered baking sheet.
5. Let rise again. Brush the top of each bun with egg. Make a cross on each bun with a sharp knife.

6. Bake in a hot oven (400° F) for 20 minutes.
7. Remove from oven and brush the crosses with confectioner's sugar moistened with milk.

Hot cross buns, hot cross buns,
One a penny, two a penny,
Hot cross buns.

"Holy Saturday" of "Easter Eve" marks the end of morning for Jesus. At many churches there is a midnight service where candles are lit in celebration of the announcement "Christ has risen." After the service, people return home to enjoy an Easter feast. *Mayiritsa*, a rich soup made from lamb, eggs, rice and dill, is enjoyed in many Greek homes.

Jesus Christ is risen today. Hallelujah, He is risen indeed. Hallelujah.

These words are the ancient greeting and response used by Christians to greet one another on Easter Day. Many churches have brought this greeting back into practice. It is usually followed by this glorious hymn:

Jesus Christ is risen today,

Alleluia.

Our triumphant holy day,

Alleluia.

Who died once upon the cross,

Alleluia.

Suffer to redeem our loss,

Alleluia.

There are many and varied traditions associated with this day. One of the most well-known symbols of Easter is the egg. Early Christians saw the egg as a representation of Jesus' birth and gave it as an Easter gift. Often the eggs were brought to the church to be blessed before being given away, and in many areas, this is still the case.

Eggs also were regarded as symbolic of the Resurrection because they hold the germ of new life. Now they are used in modern Easter festivals and are dyed bright colours to suggest joy.

Some of the loveliest of coloured eggs are *pysanky*, the elaborately designed and decorated Ukrainian Easter eggs.

My dear friend, Olga, makes these delicate treasures each year and try as I might, my eggs are never as lovely as hers. It takes patience and a very steady hand, and Olga seems to have more of both than do I.

For those of you who have not seen one of these artworks, let me explain briefly how it is done.

You begin with a large or extra-large white chicken egg. With a pencil, lightly draw the desired design. There are a number of basic symbols, such as a triangle (representing the trinity), diamonds (knowledge), a rose (love and caring), wheat (good health) or fish (Christianity).

Heat the head of the *kistka* (or stylus) in a candle flame, and scoop up a little beeswax into the funnel. Reheat until the wax melts. Apply wax using a fine *kistka* on the fine lines, and a larger *kistka* to fill in larger areas of the design. The dye will not colour the egg where you have applied the wax. Dip the egg into the first colour (dye sequence should be from lighter to darker colours). Continue adding the wax and dipping the egg in the dyes.

When the colouring is completed, hold the egg near the side of a candle until the wax looks wet. Then pat it off with clean tissue. When the wax has been removed, you may varnish the egg and sit it on a rack to dry. The egg is then "blown" out using an egg blower or a syringe.

The result can be spectacular! If you should ever be at the Ukrainian Museum of Canada in Saskatoon, Saskatchewan, you can see exquisite examples of this fine old art form.

I now cherish the eggs that Olga has made for me even more because I understand the time and the skill needed to produce them.

The Jewish celebration of *Pesach*, or Passover, is the festival of freedom held each year at this time to commemorate the freedom and exodus of the Israelites from Egypt. It is a time of family gatherings and lavish meals called *Seders*, where the story of the Passover is retold through the reading of the *Haggadah*, the book of Exodus.

The Seder is the most important event in the Passover celebration. Usually the whole family and their friends gather together to enjoy this meal that is steeped in long-held traditions and customs.

Many years ago my husband, George, and I were invited, along with our girls, to partake in the Seder at the home of Rabbi Rosenthal and his family. What better way could there be to learn of others' beliefs?

The dinner itself is both a meal and a service of worship. The table is set with special dishes used just for the event. The centrepiece is the Seder plate with five dishes containing foods that remind us of the Israelites' struggles in their quest for freedom. Parsley dipped in salt water is a reminder of spring and the tears shed for the Israelite slaves; *charoset*, a mix of walnuts, wine, cinnamon and apple represents the mortar that the Jewish slaves used to assemble the bricks of the Pharaoh's home; bitter herbs symbolize the bitter affliction of slavery; a roasted egg, a symbol of new life and fertility; a shank bone is symbolic of the sacrificial lamb.

There are four questions asked at the Seder, and in answering these questions the story of the Jews' deliverance is told.

As well, four glasses of wine are poured which represent freedom, deliverance, redemption and release. A fifth glass is poured for the prophet Elijah and, as well, the front door is left open in order to welcome Elijah should he come to dinner.

After dinner, all of the children are sent to look for a broken piece of matzo, or *afikomen*, that is hidden before the meal begins.

At the Rosenthal dinner Rabbi Seth broke the matzo into many pieces so that each child could find a piece and receive a special gift.

Our girls found it very interesting that the whole story of the Exodus was explained by reading the *Haggadauh* aloud, rather like being part of a drama played out around a dinner table.

George and I were grateful for the opportunity to build understanding between our two families.

We all enjoyed the Passover Cheese Balls, which are easily made following this recipe.

Passover Cheese Balls

1/2 lb. cottage cheese

2 eggs, separated

2 tbsp. sugar (optional)

1/2 tsp. salt (if you don't use the sugar)

4 tbsp. (or more) matzo meal

2 tbsp. butter, melted

1. Beat egg whites until stiff.

2. Mix cheese, yolks and sugar or salt. Stir in enough matzo meal to make batter thick enough to work with your hands. Fold in butter and egg whites. Let stand 1/2 hour.

3. Make small balls and drop into boiling water. When they rise to the top they are done.

4. Serve with apple sauce, sugar and cinnamon, or sour cream.

For our friends of the Baha'i faith, a twelve-day festival called *Ridvan* (pronounced *Rizwan*) is the holiest time of the year. Celebrated from April 21 to May 2, it is the time for Baha'is to ponder the importance of their faith. On the first, ninth, and twelfth days of Ridvan, work is suspended and children do not attend school.

An American tradition in the month of April has found its way to Canada. Arbour Day, on April 22nd, honours J. Sterling Morton, who back in 1855 promoted the idea of planting trees in his nearly barren state of Nebraska. On April 22nd of that year nearly one million trees were planted. His idea was a popular one and now many communities across the United States and Canada choose this day to plant ceremonial trees and shrubs.

In our family we have our own version of Arbour Day as each grandchild and great-grandchild plants a sapling somewhere on the family property. Over the years our trees have grown and each of the children are is well aware of which trees are "theirs."

May

A delicate fabric of bird song
Floats in the air.
The smell of wet wild earth
Is everywhere.

Red small leaves of the maple
Are clenched like a hand.
Like girls at their first communion
The pear trees stand.

Oh I must pass nothing by
Without loving it much,
The raindrop I try with my lips,
The grass with my touch;

For how can I be sure
I shall see again
The world on the first of May
Shining after the rain?

Sara Teasdale wrote these lovely words to welcome
the month of May. This month holds many celebrations, but for me, May is tulips, daffodils and lilacs.
I welcome them all.

The May Day celebration on May 1st really carries on an old pagan ceremony. For the Romans, the celebration was to honour Maia, the Roman goddess. Druids held their feast of Bel (or Baal of the Old Testament) on May 1st, and for many centuries the Irish and Scottish Highlanders called the festival Beltane, or Bel's Fire, when fires were lit to honour Bel.

In England, May Day was a rite-of-passage custom that marked an important seasonal transition in the year. It became very picturesque. People would head out into the woods early in the morning and return with flowering boughs of hawthorn and a growing tree, which would be set up on the village green as the Maypole.

In Victorian times, the Maypole was decorated with ribbons and the young girls of the village would dance around it.

There is an old poem that goes:

The fair maid who, the first of May,

Goes to the fields at break of day

And washes in the dew from the hawthorn tree

Will ever after handsome be.

Many of the village maidens would be sure to use the May dew in hopes that they would be more

April - Easter
The Easter celebration is the basis of Christianity—the belief in life after death.

May - Mother's Day
The earliest Mother's day celebrations can be traced back to ancient Greece and the spring festival in honour of Rhea, the Mother of the Gods.

June - St. Jean Baptiste Day
St. Jean Baptiste Day, also known as *La Fête National*, is an official holiday in the Province of Quebec.

April - Easter

May - Mother's Day

June - St. Jean Baptiste Day

beautiful and perhaps be chosen "Queen of the May," an honour that was sought after by all of the young ladies.

Here in Canada, Acadians and Québécois collect the dew, called *l'eau de mai*, on May 1st because tradition says that this water has special powers to heal and beautify.

A big part of the May Day celebration in England was a dance competition of "Morris Dancers." To this day, Morris Dancers, dressed in white shirts and pants, wear bells tied on their legs and carry large white handkerchiefs to emphasize the movements of the old and intricate English folk dances.

This old dance tradition has carried over to Canada, and in many cities including Toronto, London, Ottawa and Vancouver, the Morris Teams, as they are known, gather before dawn to "dance the sun up."

Many years ago, French-Canadians used to set up the Maypole, but this tradition is now pretty much restricted to Vancouver Island, where people of British descent keep the custom alive.

Some Europeans celebrate May 1st as Labour Day. In Canada, many German-Canadians remember this date as Labour Day, and special celebrations are held at their clubs.

For Finnish-Canadians, May 1st is *Vappu* or Carnival Day. Usually held in a hall decorated with streamers and balloons, *Vappu* is a time for drinking *sima*, a lemon-flavoured drink, and eating *tippaleipa*, a sweet bread, while dancing with friends and family. Originally, Carnival Day was linked with the labour movement and the partying of university students. It is now a social event for all to enjoy.

Some years ago, I was a patient at St. Joseph's Hospital in Toronto. There were a number of nurses involved in my care, but I was especially fond of Maria, a young Filipino girl with jet black hair and sparkling eyes.

One evening, Maria came on her shift looking particularly beautiful and cheerful. She explained that she had spent the day at Harbourfront, in downtown Toronto, in celebration of Santa Cruzan Day. When I confessed that I did not know anything about Santa Cruzan, she was happy to enlighten me.

In her native Philippines, May 3rd is the first day of spring. As well, in the Catholic Church, it is the Day of Commemoration of the Holy Cross, or Santa Cruzan. As the story goes, on this day in the fourth century A.D., the site of the crucifixion and burial of Christ was found by the Emperor Constantine. On this site, Constantine built the Church of the Holy Sepulchre and he granted freedom of worship to Christians.

In Toronto, the Filipino community organizes a spring festival and a parade, which is held at Harbourfront. Many of the participants in the parade wear costumes depicting Emperor Constantine and Queen Helena.

Young Filipino women wear their best dresses and are escorted by the most eligible bachelors.

It is a happy combination of religion and good fun.

If you have ever been in Ottawa at this time of year, you will have seen a spectacular sight on Parliament Hill. Hundreds of thousands of tulips bloom each spring, and they are a reminder of our special ties to Holland. During the Second World War, Princess Juliana of the Netherlands lived in Ottawa. As a token of their appreciation for the safety of their future monarch, the Dutch people sent four million tulip bulbs to Ottawa.

Canada has another Second World War tie with Holland. On May 5th, German forces in the Netherlands, surrendered to the Allies. The Canadian Armed Forces played a huge role in the liberation. People were starving when the Allies reached Holland, and it was the Canadians who brought food and freedom to most of the country just in time.

When Douglas How, a former war correspondent, returned to Holland in 1984 he said that "the liberation of Holland alone, it comes to me, may well be the most lasting and meaningful triumph in the history of Canadian Arms."

Dutch-Canadians celebrate Liberation Day each May 5th, and on the twenty-fifth anniversary, in 1970, they presented a baroque concert in Ottawa.

I have a personal note to add to the story. My cousin, Jack Northgrave, was one of "our boys" who gave his life near Nijmegen in Holland. Those tulips have a special meaning for our family.

St. George's Day is celebrated by Bulgarian and Macedonian-Canadians on the weekend nearest to May 6th. Very little is known about the life of St. George, but it is believed that he was born in Cappadocia, Asia Minor, and died in Lydda, Palestine, about the year A.D. 300.

According to one legend, which has its setting in Northern Africa, a princess was about to be devoured by a dragon when St. George came to her rescue and slew the dragon. His act of bravery won many converts to Christianity.

St. George is quite easily recognized, as there are many drawings and stained glass windows in his honour. He is usually depicted wearing a suit of armour with a white tunic and a red cross. Riding a horse, sword raised, he is most often shown slaying the dragon.

His red cross is also widely seen: it is the symbol for the International Red Cross, and is a part of the Union Jack.

St. George is also a popular saint in the Greek community, and many young Greek men are named for him. Do you need a little good luck? It is tradition to pull on the ears of men named George on St. George's Day, celebrated April 23rd in the Greek community.

If you should be in Toronto the fifth Sunday after Easter, you would have the chance to share in a unique experience. At St. Mary's Roman Catholic Church, situated in Portugal Square on Adelaide Street, thousands of Portuguese-Canadians (and Portuguese-Americans) celebrate Santo Cristo. The festival of Santo Cristo at St. Mary's, the largest of its kind in North America, is a tribute to a miracle said to have occurred in the Azores Islands more than 500 years ago. People praying to a statue of Jesus, which showed mysterious signs of life, seemed to be miraculously cured, much as the pilgrims who visit Lourdes in France.

The streets surrounding the church are decorated for the occasion, and the celebrations include a parade, with a statue of Christ that is carried from the church throughout the streets, marching bands, clergy, children in angel costumes, and many faithful followers carrying candles.

Mass is held outdoors at a nearby park, and afterwards, the statue is returned to the church.

When the Mass is complete, the festival becomes more carnival-like in atmosphere, with games, rides, Portuguese food and partying into the night.

It is really a very special chance to partake in a part of Catholic Portuguese history.

The earliest Mother's Day celebrations can be traced back to ancient Greece and the spring festival in honour of Rhea, the Mother of the Gods. England celebrated "Mothering Sunday" way back in the 1600s. Many of England's poor worked as servants in wealthy homes, often living in the houses of their employers, located far from their own homes. On "Mothering Sunday," servants were given the day off and encouraged to return home and spend the day with their mothers. A special cake called the "Mothering cake" provided a festive touch to the occasion.

In 1872, Julia Ward Howe (author of the lyrics to "The Battle Hymn of the Republic") suggested Mother's Day as a day dedicated to peace.

In 1907, Anna Jarvis, of Philadelphia, began a campaign to establish a national Mother's Day. So successful was her quest that President Woodrow Wilson, in 1914, proclaimed Mother's Day as a national holiday to be held each year on the second Sunday in May.

Although I have received many lovely tributes over the years, I believe my favourite came from the girls many years ago. The three of them took a basket out into a field near our home and picked a lovely bouquet of wild flowers. With it came a paper card with a note carefully printed in Margaret's best Grade One printing, and signed by all three girls. Given with hugs and kisses, I cherish the memory of that Mother's Day morning so long ago.

We can only have one mother,
Patient, kind and true,
No other friend in all the world,
Will be so true to you;
For all her loving kindness,
She asks nothing in return;
If all the world deserts you,
To your mother you can turn.

We can only have one mother,
No one else can take her place;
You can't tell how much you'll need her,
'Til you miss her loving face.
Be careful how you answer her,
Choose every word you say,
Remember she's your mother,
Tho' now she's old and grey.

We can only have one mother,
Oh, take her to your heart.
You cannot tell how soon the time,
When you and she must part.
Let her know you love her dearly,
Cheer and comfort her each day,
You can never get another,
When she has passed away.

On the seventh Sunday after Easter, those of us of the Christian faith celebrate the day of Pentecost, or Whitsunday. This is the day when we give thanks for the gift of the Holy Spirit to the Apostles. In Jesus' words, "I will not leave you desolate . . . I will come to you."

Pentecost is often a time for baptisms. The choice of white clothing worn at the baptismal service gave rise to the name "White Sunday," or Whitsun in old English.

Another celebration of Pentecost takes place on the fiftieth day after the beginning of Passover. Called *Shavu'ot* or the "Feast of the Weeks," it is the Jewish holiday celebrating the harvest season in the Holy Land.

Shavu'ot also commemorates the anniversary of Moses and the Israelites receiving the Torah and the Ten Commandments at Mount Sinai.

There are many traditions and customs of Shavu'ot, and they have evolved from the legends and stories describing the experiences of the Israelites at Mount Sinai. One story says that the Israelites overslept on the morning of Shavu'ot. To compensate for this negligence, many Jews stay awake from dusk to dawn, reading from the Torah and the Talmud.

Another Shavu'ot custom is the eating of dairy products. Perhaps this tradition came from a passage in the Torah which reads; "And He gave us this land, a land flowing with milk and honey."

Some people celebrate Shavu'ot by eating blintzes, cheesecakes or other dairy dishes. I confess that cheese blintzes are a favourite of mine, and this recipe is particularly delicious.

Cheese Blintzes

Batter:

4 eggs

1 cup milk

1 cup flour

1 tbsp. sour cream

1/4 cup sugar

1 package of vanilla sugar

pinch of salt

oil for frying

Filling:

16 oz. cottage cheese

2 egg yolks

2 tbsp. sugar

2 tbsp. margarine or butter, melted

1/4 cup raisins (optional)

1. *Batter:* Combine eggs and milk. Add sour cream and blend well. Add flour gradually. Mix well until batter is smooth.

2. Heat a small amount of oil in an 8-inch frying pan until hot but not smoking. Ladle a small amount of batter into the pan, tipping the pan in all directions until the batter covers the entire bottom of the pan.

3. Fry on one side until set and golden (about one minute). Slip the pancake out of the pan and repeat until all of the batter is used, adding oil as necessary.

4. *Filling:* Mix all the ingredients for the filling together.

5. *To assemble*: Fill each pancake on the golden side with three tablespoons of filling. Fold in the sides to the centre and roll the blintz until it is completely closed. Replace the blintzes in the pan and fry for two minutes, turning once.

Cheese blintzes are served hot with sour cream or applesauce. (I like them with both!)

Wesak is the most important day for members of the Buddhist faith. Coming on the full moon, it marks the triple celebration of the Buddha's Birth, Enlightenment and Final Demise.

Many of the Buddhists in Canada have come from central and eastern Asia, and live in the larger Canadian cities of Vancouver, Montreal and Toronto. *Wesak* celebrations in these cities often include various Buddhist rituals, prayers and meditation. It is believed that meditation brings enlightenment, which allows the attainment of nirvana, where one is free from ignorance, desire and hatred.

We who were born in Canada, and those who have made Canada their chosen country, have a day in May to reflect on our rights and duties, privileges and responsibilities as citizens of this wonderful country.

The Citizenship Act came into force on January 1, 1947, and the federal government proclaimed the first "Citizenship Day" on May 23, 1950. In 1955, it was declared that Citizenship Day would be the Friday preceding the Victoria Day celebration.

Although our country is something that many of us take for granted, we would be wise to remember just how lucky we are to live here.

Queen Victoria, the late British monarch, was born on May 24th in 1819. A very young woman when she became queen, she was the longest-reigning monarch in British history.

Throughout the British Empire in the last century, it was the custom to celebrate the birthday of the monarch with a holiday. As Victoria's birthday was celebrated for such a long time, it was made a permanent holiday, and, since 1952, Victoria Day has been celebrated on the Monday preceding May 24th.

For many people, this is the first long weekend of the summer season and, in many areas, it is the weekend to open up the cottage.

In Victoria, the city named for the monarch, the festivities go well beyond the usual fireworks displays held in the rest of the country.

Parades, concerts, and a sail-past in the harbour are just a few of the events held to honour a very special monarch.

At the Six Nations reserve near Brantford, Ontario, Bread and Cheese Day is celebrated on Victoria Day. Since 1837, it has been the practice to distribute bread and cheese to the residents of the reserve. The custom was begun by agents of Queen Victoria. Now it is the Six Nations band councillors who distribute the bread and cheese from the community centre. It is also an occasion for cultural displays and for such special occasions such as ball games, horse racing, singing and dancing.

Blossom Time, for many of us the most eagerly awaited time of the year, is the most fleeting. However, even a brief glimpse of pale pink and white blossoms is a welcome respite from the drab greys and browns of winter's end.

Although there are many blossom festivals in areas across Canada (notably in Creston, B.C., and Niagara Falls, Ontario), one of the longest running and best-known festival is the Annapolis Valley Apple Blossom Festival.

Since the 1930s, Canadians and Americans have been trekking to the Kentville-Grand Pré area of Nova Scotia to enjoy the delicately scented blossoms of about a million apple trees, along with a parade, barbecues, sports events and the crowning of Queen Annapolisa, the queen of the festival.

HERITAGE FAMILY TRADITIONS

Americans who are now living in Canada set aside a day each year to remember departed friends and family members, particularly those who were lost in the wars.

Time cannot steal the treasures
That we carry in our hearts,
Nor ever dim the shining thoughts
Our cherished past imparts.
And memories of the ones we've loved
Still cast their gentle glow,
To grace our days and light our paths
Wherever we may go.

June

And what is so rare as a day in June?
Then, if ever, come perfect days;
Then heaven tries earth, if it be in tune,
And over it softly her warm ear lays;
Whether we look, or whether we listen,
We hear life murmur, or see it glisten,
Every clod feels a stir of might,
An instinct within it that reaches and towers,
And grasping blindly above it for light,
Clings to a soul in grass and flowers.

James Russell Lowell

I am happy to welcome this month that will give us summer. There are a number of special celebrations in this month, but some of you may not be old enough to remember this particular commemoration.

The first or second Sunday in June was once Memorial Day, known in some areas as Decoration Sunday. This tradition was kept long before the days of commercial cemeteries or crematoriums. At this time, the cemetery was kept either by a church or a small community. There were no endowment funds to pay for a cemetery caretaker. As soon as the crops were sown, and the gardens planted, there would be a "cleaning bee" where families would work to tidy up the cemetery, cutting the grass and planting annuals on the graves of their forebears. Then, on the first or second Sunday in June, there would be an appropriate memorial service in the cemetery with a village band and guest clergy coming to preach.

It was always followed by a special supper, either in the church basement or at a parishioner's home. It was a time of renewing old friendships as neighbours and relatives came together.

This tradition is still carried on in some small or remote communities across Canada.

Early in June, or July depending on geography and weather, churches of many denominations hold a "Strawberry Social." More often than not, these festivals are fundraisers, but all of them are an opportunity to enjoy this delicious fruit and the camaraderie of family and friends.

Many years ago, my family all were fortunate enough to attend the Terra Nova Strawberry Festival in Southern Ontario. My daughters liked to eat until they were over full, but they never seemed to be aware that there were any other dishes being served except for the wonderful pies and cakes that the ladies provided.

In Manitoba, where the strawberries come a little later, Canada's National Strawberry Festival is one of central Manitoba's premier events. Held in Portage la Prairie in late June or early July, it features activities for all ages and, as well, it includes aboriginal shows and a giant flea market.

The Iroquois celebrate a Strawberry Festival that is a time to give thanks for the "first fruits" and to herald summer's arrival.

A beautiful part of this thanksgiving is the performance of the "Great Feather Dance," the dance that is also a part of the Midwinter Festival.

After the Fascist regime came to an end in Italy in 1945, Victor Emmanuel, the very unpopular king, attempted to save the monarchy by abdicating in favour of his son. He was unsuccessful, and on June 2nd, the Italian people voted in favour of a Republic.

In Canada, National Day is celebrated on the first Sunday in June, with a reception at the consulate and speeches in the Italian communities.

In Canada's westernmost province, British Columbia, a double celebration takes place June 13th. On this date in 1792, Captain George Vancouver, leaving his ships moored in Birch Bay, rowed with his men in small boats into Burrard Inlet, where he discovered the site which now bears his name. Then, on the same day in 1886, the small settlement was burned right to the water's edge. The people wasted no time, however, in planning a new and even greater city. Today, Vancouver is the largest city in British Columbia and the shipping capital of western Canada.

The third Sunday in June is a day to honour the "King" of the household—Father's Day. How well I remember my own father. He was a man of principle and honour. He set high standards and lived his life by them. What a truly fine example he set for us children, and how well he brought us to adulthood with his warmth and his love.

Mrs. John B. Dodd of Washington was the first to propose the idea of "Father's Day" in 1910. William Smart, her father and a Civil War veteran, was widowed when his wife (Mrs. Dodd's mother) died while giving birth to their sixth child. Mr. Smart was left to raise the baby and the other five children by himself on a rural farm in eastern Washington state. It was only after she became an adult that Mrs. Dodd realized the strength of character her father had shown raising six children as a single parent.

Father's Day was first observed in Spokane on June 19, 1910. In 1924, President Calvin Coolidge supported the idea of a national Father's Day. Finally, in 1966, President Lyndon B. Johnson signed a presidential proclamation declaring the third Sunday in June as Father's Day.

Here in Canada, we have followed the American lead and also celebrate the day on the third Sunday each June.

Somewhere between June 20 and 22, summer begins in Canada with the summer solstice. This is the longest day of the year, and the further north you go, the more daylight hours you will enjoy.

Early in our marriage, George and I spent a year in Canada's Far North. It was an enormous learning experience for both of us, but my strongest memory is of celebrating the summer solstice with a twenty-four-hour party. In the area where the sun never sets on this day, the people took full advantage of the light to hold a celebration that included the entire community. We played softball, we had games and races, we had a gigantic pot luck supper, and after supper we danced for hours. We were very tired the next day but the sense of fun and joy that we shared remains in my memory to this day.

Many areas in Canada welcome the summer solstice with celebrations or festivals.

From Newfoundland, where bonfires are lit near St. Mary's Bay, to Whistler Village, British Columbia, where there is a Scandinavian Midsummer Festival, all of us welcome the summer and the warm and sunny days that it brings.

One of Korea's great national holidays is celebrated here in Canada. The *Dano* Festival, held on the fifth day of the fifth moon, features wrestling contests for young men and swinging contests for young women. It is a kind of summer festival giving particular recognition to women.

Chinese-Canadians also have a celebration near the fifth day of the fifth moon on the Chinese calendar.

The Dragon Boat Festival honours an ancient Chinese poet and statesman, Qu Yuan, who drowned himself in protest against political corruption and injustice. Legend has it that as the townspeople tried to rescue him, they beat drums and splashed their oars to frighten away the fish and water dragons. To keep the fish from eating Qu Yuan's body, the fishermen threw a kind of dumpling made from rice and meat and other ingredients wrapped in bamboo leaves into the river.

Today, festival activities recall the legendary events. Participants in the boat races eat the dumplings made from glutinous rice, which have been wrapped in leaves and tied with threads: green, red, yellow, white and black. They are eaten on the day of the Dragon Boat Festival to honour Qu Yuan.

To symbolize attempts to rescue Qu Yuan, participants race elaborately decorated, narrow "dragon" boats. These boats measure twelve metres and have ornately carved and painted "dragon" heads and tails, and each boat carries a crew of twenty-two paddlers.

Here in Canada, the Canadian International Dragon Boat Festival, held in Vancouver, is a truly unique event. At the Plaza of Nations, on the shores of False Creek, there is a three-day presentation of the performing and visual arts with performers drawn from the professional and semi-professional arts community of Canada, with special guests from Pacific Rim countries.

Add to this a culinary festival featuring foods of the world, and the dragon boat races themselves, held in the east basin of False Creek, and you have a true multicultural event.

Just as people lit fires in ancient times to strengthen the weakening sun at winter solstice, so, too, did they light "midsummer fires" to help keep the sun strong.

Later, as Christianity spread in Europe, the fires became known as St. John's Fires, heralding St. John's Day, June 24th. Many European-Canadians still light midsummer fires to celebrate the solstice.

Danish-Canadians hold their celebration for St. Hans Day out in the country on the eve of the 24th. They light a huge bonfire for the burning of a "witch" and there is singing, dancing and partying.

Poles also light bonfires on midsummer's eve (*Sobotka*) and set candlelit wreaths afloat on rivers and streams.

Many groups in Canada celebrate Midsummer's Day, which is also known as St. John's Day. Some Swedish midsummer festivals include a Maypole and many traditional dancers.

Latvian-Canadians call June 24th St. John's Day, and like many other groups, they celebrate with picnics and bonfires.

The greatest celebration of this day takes place in the province of Quebec. St. Jean Baptiste is the patron saint of French-Canadians. Traditionally, a saint is honoured by the church on his death. St. Jean Baptiste is the exception to this rule, as he was consecrated in his mother's womb, when the Virgin Mary, great with child, entered the house of Elizabeth.

There are parades in many areas of the province, and often there is a float that features St. Jean as a young shepherd with a pet lamb. The lamb is woolly and white with a bow tied around its neck.

In the city of Montreal, the festivities are many and varied. Through the years, there have been musical revues, featuring leading artists in the province; a Gala featuring band competitions, choral music and folk dancing; a Mass on the square in front of Notre Dame Church; and the Guillaume Couture Oratorio, *Jean le Precurseur,* at Place des Arts.

The night before, on the 23rd, there is a "Communion of Bonfires" all along the banks of the St. Lawrence River. One town begins with its fire and this is the signal for the next town or village to light its fire. The fires travel on both sides of the St. Lawrence River, all the way to the Ontario border. Also called "Fires of Joy," they are part of a long-lasting custom that came to Canada with the early French-Canadian settlers.

St. Jean Baptiste Day is also known as *La Fête National* and is an official holiday in the Province of Quebec.

In many of the smaller towns and villages, this is a day for family get-togethers, where picnic dinners are enjoyed with fireworks being a part of the evening celebrations.

One of the most popular dishes enjoyed by the Québécois is the meat pie, *la tourtière*. My dear friend, Madeleine Pouliot, sends this recipe for her family pie.

Tourtière (Meat Pie)

1 onion

1 clove garlic, minced

1/2 tsp. salt

1/2 tsp. savoy or thyme

1/4 tsp. celery salt

1/4 tsp. ground cloves

1/2 cup water

1. In a pot, mix together the beef and pork and add the other ingredients.
2. Bring all ingredients to a boil.

3. Turn down to simmer for 20 minutes.

4. Add 1/4 cup bread crumbs spoon by spoon until the fat is absorbed.

5. Cool the mixture. Pour into an uncooked pie shell. Add the top crust.

6. Cook 25 minutes in a preheated 450° F oven.

St. Jean Baptiste Day is an important celebration in francophone communities across our country.

It's also an interesting fact that St. John's, Newfoundland, was given its name because it was on the eve of St. John's Day that explorer John Cabot sailed into the harbour in 1497. This day in Newfoundland is called Discovery Day.

My sister Sarah has an unusual story about Discovery Day in Newfoundland. This comes from the Micmac Indians.

The Indians say that when the Manitou, the Great Spirit, was making the continent of the New World, he found that he had much material left over in the shape of rocks, swamps and useless trees. So he formed a big rubbish heap by casting it all into the sea to the northeast, and called it *Wee-soc-Kadao*. Several years later, Cabot discovered and claimed the island for Great Britain, and called it Newfoundland.

St. John's Day, St. Jean Baptiste Day or Discovery Day, all are important to us as Canadians from coast to coast.

On the last weekend in June, members of the many German-Canadian organizations are invited to a congress in Kitchener, Ontario. Called "Sommerfest," the congress is combined with performances of gymnastics, dancing and singing. Canadians of many cultural origins attend Sommerfest and it offers a chance to build good sportsmanship and lasting friendships.

Although Hindus now live in many parts of the world, their major cultural heritage is Indian. Hindus believe in one Supreme God, but they also believe that God can have many forms. Most Hindu festivals celebrate events in the lives of their gods, especially Krishna and Rama.

Ratha Yatra, the famous "Festival of the Chariots," is held in late June or early July to honour Jagannath, Lord of the Universe.

In Puri, India, the deities are taken from the temple and placed in decorated chariots. They are taken on a symbolic journey three kilometres down Puri's Grand Road.

Similar festive carts are taken out in Montreal, Toronto, and Vancouver. The *Ratha Yatra* ceremony draws a large crowd of worshippers, many of whom come from the Hare Krishna movement.

There is a festival on Canada's East Coast that is of historical significance. In fact, this celebration takes place in Madawaska, Maine, but it also involves Acadians, who live in the Edmunston area of New Brunswick, on the Maine border.

The Madawaska Territory at one time ran along the Canadian border between Maine and New Brunswick, and was settled by a group of thirteen families, farmers who were chased out of Acadia by the English in the late eighteenth century. As these settlements expanded, they eventually separated into Canadian and American communities, with Edmunston in New Brunswick and Madawaska and St. David on the American side of the St. John River.

In 1978, the Madawaska historical society proclaimed June 28th as Acadian Day in the state of Maine. Since then, it has been the site of a French-Canadian festival lasting anywhere from one day to one week. Events at the festival include French music and dancing and an Acadian supper featuring *pot en pot* and *fougere*. There is also a parade, with bands and marching groups from Maine and New Brunswick. Following an Acadian Mass, there is a procession to the white marble cross that identifies the site of the Acadian settlement.

My sister, Sarah, and her husband, Richard, enjoyed this festival several years ago. They said that it was a wonderful occasion with Canadians and Americans alike enjoying delicious food and a spirit of camaraderie that erased the border between our countries.

July

In 1864, representatives from New Brunswick, Nova Scotia, Quebec and Ontario met in Charlottetown, Prince Edward Island, to consider confederation. After some three years of discussions and compromises, confederation became reality. On July 1st, 1867, the British North America Act proclaimed "the Provinces . . . into one Dominion" under the name of Canada. The B.N.A. Act was renamed the Constitution Act and was patriated in September of 1981.

Canada Day is celebrated all across the country by every one of us who needs a chance to say how much we love to be here. Picnics, parades and fireworks displays are the most common ways to celebrate, but there are hundreds of uncommon celebrations as well.

In Victoria, B.C., there are multicultural concerts; in Kamloops, B.C., there is a giant birthday cake and games for the children.

In Edmonton, Alberta, there is an annual Canada Day fifteen-kilometre road race along with citizenship court sessions and a multicultural dance extravaganza. People in Banff enjoy sidewalk art, face painting and a Canada Day breakfast.

The village of Findlater, Saskatchewan, has volleyball games, tree and flower plantings, horseshoe competitions, races and a barbecue.

In Eston, Saskatchewan, there is the "World Championship Gopher Derby." Sixty-four of these burrowing rodents are captured, named (as you would name thoroughbred horses) and raced at the fairgrounds.

In Gimli, Manitoba, the national anthem is sung in English, Ukrainian, and Icelandic, and cultural events are enjoyed by all.

In Ontario, the largest celebration is in the nation's capital, Ottawa. A flag-raising ceremony, the Changing of the Guard, The R.C.M.P. musical ride, and speeches by the Governor General and by the Prime Minister all take place on Parliament Hill as a prelude to a spectacular fireworks display. There are other events to be enjoyed, staged in parks and recreation areas all over the city.

Montreal, Quebec, often presents musical fireworks displays featuring Canadian heritage themes.

Dawson City, in the Yukon Territory, features the Yukon Gold Panning Championships, which often coincide with Canada Day celebrations.

The East Coast celebrations include a lighted boat parade in Fredericton, New Brunswick, a military fly-by in Halifax, Nova Scotia, Scottish highland dancing in Summerside, P.E.I., and a sunrise ceremony in Cornerbrook, Newfoundland.

In whichever province you live, there are literally hundreds of ways to celebrate our unity "from sea to sea."

The story of our national anthem, an integral part of Canada Day celebrations, is an interesting one. In 1880, when "O Canada" was composed, the country was still dependent on Britain and the anthem was "God Save the Queen." In spring of that year, the St. Jean Baptiste Society of Quebec organized a festival for French-speaking people from all across North America. The music committee of the society decided that a song was needed.

Calixa Lavallée, a Quebec musician, composed the music and Adolph-Basile Routhier wrote the verses in French. The official premiere was June 24th, St. Jean Baptiste Day, 1880.

In 1908, in a competition organized by *Colliers Weekly,* the words of Robert Stanley Weir came to be those of the official English anthem.

In 1967, the words were amended to those which we now sing with love and enthusiasm.

O Canada! Our home and native land!

True patriot love, in all thy sons command,

With glowing hearts we see thee rise,

The True North strong and free!

From far and wide, O Canada,

We stand on guard for thee.

God, keep our land, glorious and free!

O Canada, we stand on guard for thee

O Canada, we stand on guard for thee!

In our family, we often make Canada Day a family reunion. Brothers, sisters, aunts, uncles, cousins— all try to come together, often at the country home of my grandson Fred and his wife June. Those of us who, like me, enjoy senior status, stay in one of the many bedrooms in the home, while the younger generations set up tents in the yard.

It's a time of renewing friendships, enjoying pot luck meals (where even the youngest can pitch in to help), and endless "family" stories that are told again and again. It celebrates our family "roots" and allows us to give the children a sense of where they have come from and to show them that, no matter where they go, family is forever.

On the Canada Day weekend, Liverpool, Nova Scotia, has its own heritage celebration known as Privateer Days.

A privateer was a ship under papers, called a "Marque of Letters," to a government or company to perform specific tasks. The men who sailed these ships were also known as privateers. During war times, these privateers would loot, pillage and plunder England's enemies. For their efforts, the monarch would reward them with a portion of the plunder and safe harbour.

Liverpool, "Port of the Privateers," has a history dating back to the colonial era of the 1700s. The Perkins House Museum and adjacent Queen's County Museum tell of the area's turbulent past.

The Privateer Days celebration, with its period costumes, barbecues, entertainment and parades, is always a well-attended event.

On the first Sunday in July, Czechs and Slovaks meet in Scarborough, Ontario, to observe Czechoslovak Day and *Sokol Slet*. (The word *sokol* means falcon and *slet* means flying together in one place.)

The Sokol organization places great importance on high moral qualities, patriotism and good citizenship. The first Sokol unit was formed in Prague in 1862, and it soon became a world-wide organization. The first Canadian unit was formed in Frank, Alberta, in 1912. Sokol Toronto began in 1931.

The Sokol program includes calisthenics, apparatus work, track and field events and certain sports. The celebrations on this day includes an ecumenical religious ceremony and wreath-laying in memory of the freedom fighters who gave their lives in the struggle for liberty.

A part of our Canadian heritage is celebrated in Saskatchewan in early July.

Louis Riel, Métis leader and leader of the "Riel Revolution" in Manitoba and Saskatchewan in 1885, is honoured on "Louis Riel Day," the day before the Saskatoon Fair and Exhibition, in Saskatchewan.

Traditional Métis skills are showcased in a race which includes running, horseback riding and canoeing.

Later in the month, Riel and the Métis and Native people who died in the rebellion are honoured at the traditional "Feast of the Dead." This service is held on the Métis lands near Batoche National Historic Site, north of Saskatoon. It is the culmination of ten days of activities that include ball tournaments, music festivals, fiddling and jigging contests and a Native rodeo.

Throughout the summer months, Croatian-Canadians enjoy "Croatian Days," usually a community get-together in the form of a picnic and a cultural program. It's a wonderful way to delight in our beautiful summer weather.

Irish-Canadians commemorate the battle of the Boyne, which took place in 1690, with celebrations sponsored by the Orange Order. "The Glorious Twelfth" celebration is often a parade led by a symbolic King William III riding on a grey horse.

The early settlers in our country needed special skills, and these skills are celebrated at the Calgary Stampede in Calgary, Alberta.

Often called the greatest outdoor show on earth, it attracts the world's top professional cowboys, who compete for hundreds of thousands of dollars during the ten-day event.

The Stampede was begun in 1912 by a young cowboy from Wyoming, Guy Weadick, who dreamed of gathering the finest crew of bronco busters and offering them enormous purses in competition.

Weadick's dream has grown to become Canada's largest rodeo.

If you have never seen a rodeo, you have really missed a spectacular event. I have been lucky enough to attend the Calgary Stampede on many occasions, and each time I enjoy myself even more. It is difficult to imagine how skilled the cowboys are until you see them at work. They can compete in saddle bronc and bareback riding, steer wrestling, calf roping, bull riding and—my favourite—the chuckwagon race.

There are many other things to see and do, including visiting the Wild West town of Weadickville, or an Indian village that is populated by groups from five Indian tribes, a Frontier Casino with blackjack table and roulette wheels, and agricultural and livestock exhibits.

The people of Calgary are so warm and friendly! Each person seems to feel that it is his or her personal responsibility to ensure that you enjoy your stay in their beautiful city. A visit to the Calgary Stampede can give you a look into the early years of the West.

Japanese Buddhists celebrate a most important festival July 13 to 15. *O-Bon*, sometimes known as the "Festival of Lanterns for the Dead" focuses on keeping the memory of ancestors alive. It is believed that their spirits return each year to visit the family and, to honour them, a special meal of vegetables, rice and fruit is set out. Lighted lanterns welcome them and guide their return.

On the final day, July 15th, farewell dumplings are prepared and fires are lit to guide the spirits back.

The climax is the *Bon-Odori*, or "Dance of Rejoicing," folk dances performed by the light of paper lanterns to comfort the souls of the dead. It is a round dance, similar to the old May Day dances.

In Toronto, the dance is often performed at Nathan Phillips Square, at City Hall.

The *O-Bon* festival is also celebrated in the Vancouver area with the round dance and lanterns floating in the harbour, which is quite spectacular to see.

Vietnamese-Canadians call this festival *Vu Lan*, and ceremonies are held in their temples to revere their ancestors.

The Feast of the Lonesome Souls, or *Cung Co Hon*, is celebrated by the Chinese Buddhists around the same time. My grandson, Marshall, and his wife, Jamie, have close friends who are Chinese-Canadian. On several occasions, Marshall and Jamie have joined them to celebrate this important festival.

On the eve of *Cung Co Hon*, a feast is held for lonesome souls in order that these souls will do no harm. Rice, boiled chicken, fish and sweet cakes are set out for the spirits to enjoy. Of course, the family enjoys a delicious meal together and, in many families, there is a religious service celebrated at the temple. Jamie and Marshall felt honoured to be included in this ancient festival.

I love summer rain. I could sit for hours and listen to the drops as they beat upon the window. A summer rain brings to mind these lines from Robert Loveman:

The clouds of gray engulf the day
And overwhelm the town;
It is not raining rain to me,
It's raining roses down.

A health unto the happy,
A fig for him who frets!
It is not raining rain to me,
It's raining violets.

There is a legend in England that says you can predict the weather for the rest of the summer, according to the weather on July 15th. When Swithin, Bishop of Winchester, England, died in A.D. 862, he was buried, according to his wishes, outside the Cathedral. After his canonization, clerical authorities decided to move his remains to a site within the church. As the story goes, the heavens opened up and the rain poured down for forty days, a show of the saint's displeasure. This led to the popular belief that if it rains on St. Swithin's Day, it will rain for forty days, but if it is fair, it will be dry for forty days. Apparently, St. Swithin is also the patron saint of rain—or lack thereof.

In 1650, a group of sailors built a small wooden church on the site where the town of Beaupre, Quebec, now stands. It was built to honour St. Anne, who was thought to be the guardian of those who lived or worked by the sea, by a group of sailors who had been caught in a vicious storm. The men had vowed that if St. Anne saved them, they would build a shrine to her honour where they first touched land, and they were good for that pledge.

In 1658, the people of the village built a larger church and the first of St. Anne de Beaupre's supernatural cures occurred. A man who suffered from rheumatism came to worship in the church and walked away, miraculously cured.

News of the restoration to health spread quickly, and soon the infirm and the crippled began to make their way to the church hoping to be cured themselves.

Since that time, thousands of cures have been reported at the Basilica of St. Anne. The crutches, wheelchairs and braces that hang on the walls inside the beautiful building attest to these miracles.

The original chapel has been enlarged and rebuilt eight times since it was originally erected.

Known as the "Lourdes of the New World," the pilgrimage to the shrine is one of the major pilgrimages on the North American continent.

Gypsies, from all over the United States and Canada, celebrate "Santana" at the basilica. They camp on the church property and prepare a *slava*, a feast of special foods, including lamb that has been barbecued over an open fire. Each family prepares a table and everyone takes a turn eating at everyone else's table.

As the bells of the church toll, the gypsies join the other pilgrims in a candlelight parade from the church, across the road and up the hill.

Although many hundreds of people come to St. Anne in hopes of being miraculously cured, this is not a part of the gypsy tradition. For them, Santana is a reunion and a social time; a time to dance and celebrate being together again.

St. Ann (without the "*e*") is looked on as the patron saint of the Micmac natives of Nova Scotia and New Brunswick. As with the Basilica at Beaupre, St. Ann's Mission, on Chapel Island (near Cape Breton Island), is thought to be a sacred place and many Micmac families visit there hoping to be healed. On St. Ann's Day (Procession Day), July 26th, a statue of St. Ann is carried from the church and up the hill. There is an old custom that says that if you crawl on your hands and knees to the foot of the statue and kiss its feet any infirmity will be cured. This is known as "crawling to St. Ann."

Many summer festivals in Canada celebrate food. It is a time of growth and rich harvests. In our eastern province of Newfoundland there is one such festival, celebrating not something grown, but something caught. The Exploits Valley Salmon Festival is an annual event in the Grand Falls–Windsor area of central Newfoundland. This festival is a five-day event to celebrate the catch of the salmon season. There is fine dining, music and dancing, with concerts from some of Canada's best-known performers. If you enjoy salmon, you would love this mid-July festival, and the host people will go out of their way to make sure you are properly welcomed.

The Canadian plains, before Confederation, were home to many Indian bands. Buffalo were the main source of their food, clothing, blankets, etc. The buffalo bones that remained were gathered into a huge round pile. This enormous pile of bones was a monument to continued good hunting, because the Indians believed that the animals would not leave an area where the bones of other buffalo rested. The Cree name for this pile of bones was *Oksuna-Kasus-Teki*. Eventually, the name became *wascana*, from the Cree word *oksana* (bones) and also because the bone pile marked the place to cross the Wascana Creek.

HERITAGE FAMILY TRADITIONS

Mennonites in Manitoba celebrate their heritage during the last weekend in July. Members of an evangelical Protestant sect originating in Europe, the Mennonites began to emigrate to North America in the late seventeenth century. Here they lived primarily as farmers, retaining their German language and customs.

Many Russian Mennonites settled in Manitoba along the "Mennonite Trail." Because the Mennonites were the first to extract oil from the sunflower plants, the city of Altona, in southern Manitoba, celebrates its Mennonite heritage with the Sunflower Festival.

Traditional German and Russian food is served, with a special treat made especially for the festival—sunflower ice cream.

I have never had the pleasure of attending this festival, but my friend Mavis Tewsbury, who has made many visits, assures me that she would return "just for the ice cream."

August

Star-gazing is a wonderful summer evening's entertainment. For centuries, man has fixed his eyes upon the heavens and dreamed, and poets have penned immortal lines about the astral bodies. Lord Byron wrote:

Ye stars! Which are the poetry of heaven,
If in your bright leaves we could read the fate
Of men and empires—'tis to be forgiven
That in our aspirations to be great
Our destinies o'erleap their mortal state,
And claim a kindred with you; for ye are
A beauty and a mystery, and create
In us such love and reverence from afar,
That fortune, fame, power, life, have named
Themselves a star.

Tanabata, the Japanese Star Festival, is based on an ancient legend of parted lovers who are identified with the stars Altair and Vega. As the story goes, Orihime (Vega) lived with her father, the Emperor, in a palace on the east coast of the Milky Way. Vega spent her days weaving fine garments for the Emperor. She fell in love with Kengyu (Altair) and the two married. After their marriage, Vega neglected her weaving and Altair disregarded his herd. This so angered the Emperor that he separated the lovers, making them live on opposite sides of the river in heaven, as the Milky Way is known. One day each year, magpies form a bridge over the river and the two are able to meet. If it rains, the lovers must wait another year.

This celebration was traditionally held on the seventh day of the seventh moon on the lunar calendar, but, more often nowadays, on July seventh. In Canada, the ceremony may be held in late August or September, when it appears that the two stars, sparkling in the summer sky, move closer to one another.

The Japanese-Canadian Cultural Centre often celebrates the festival with Japanese dancing, judo, karate and demonstrations of weaving.

My daughter, Julia, has a job with a multinational corporation. In the course of a year, she travels quite extensively, and those of us here at home anxiously await her return so that we can enjoy her travels vicariously.

Several years ago, Julia was in Switzerland on August 1st. This is Swiss National Day, celebrating the unification of the three original cantons in 1291.

The Swiss celebrate in many ways, but one of the most interesting is the heavy-rock-throwing competition, a nineteenth-century tradition among alpine herdsmen. This competition is repeated every four years at the festival in Interlaken.

Julia was delighted to show her photos to us. Many of them were of the traditional dancers in the beautiful costumes of long ago.

After a delicious fondue dinner with friends, Julia took more photos of the magnificent fireworks display over the lake.

Here in Canada, many Swiss families enjoy an evening with friends, often singing and dancing or watching the children's *lampion* parade (*lampions* are small lamps made of red paper and often decorated with the coats of arms of the various Swiss cantons).

Although Julia has visited Switzerland many times, no trip has been as memorable as the one she took that included the national celebration.

Sometimes at the end of July or in August, our Jewish friends spend a day of feasting, prayer and mourning in memory of the destruction of both the first and second temples in Jerusalem. *Tish'ah Be'av* is also the traditional day for Jews to pause and reflect on the enormous tragedies that have befallen the Jewish people. It is a time for reflection and rediscovery of the spiritual strength necessary to face the future.

On the first weekend in August, there is a wonderful celebration of Caribbean culture that draws people from all parts of the world to the city of Toronto. "Caribana" draws a large group who return each year from the different island nations of the Caribbean, with Trinidad, Tobago and Jamaica sending the largest delegations of revellers.

Dozens of steel bands and thousands of dancers in fantastic brilliant-coloured costumes perform in front of the judges' viewing stands before heading off down Lakeshore Boulevard for a parade.

Caribana began back in 1967 as a Canadian centennial celebration for the black community who came to Canada from the West Indies. Soon, black Canadians from all backgrounds began to come to Toronto for this unique event.

Carifesta, a similar celebration, began in Montreal just a few years later.

You can be a part of these vibrant celebrations of music, art, culture and food. I know that the organizers welcome Canadians of all cultures to this wildly happy and exciting occasion.

The first weekend in August gives most of us in Canada a holiday. The first Monday is proclaimed a civic holiday in every province except Quebec. This particular holiday has no historical or religious significance, and most people enjoy the day by doing their favourite summer activities. My son-in-law, Bruce, and my grandson, Marshall, enjoy this day on a golf course. Marshall jokes that the holiday was called in his honour, as it was on the Civic Holiday a few years ago that he shot his first hole in one.

Different provinces have given this holiday names uniquely suited to their territory. In Nova Scotia, it is Natal Day, celebrating the founding of Halifax in 1749. Ontario honours its first Lieutenant-Governor, John Graves Simcoe, by calling this day "Simcoe Day." In Alberta and Saskatchewan, they celebrate "Heritage Day," and in British Columbia, people enjoy "B.C. Day."

Wherever you are, it is a time to enjoy our all-too-short, wonderful summer season.

Our country's capital city has a unique festival that runs for five days through the August Civic Holiday. The "Sparks Street Mall International Busker Festival" in Ottawa is Canada's second-largest busker festival, second only to the event hosted in Halifax. Jugglers, comedians, mimes, musicians, storytellers and magicians come from all over the world to showcase their talents. Ottawa's own "Junkyard Symphony," which makes music from old pots and pans—and even the kitchen sink—is a popular performer at this show. The trees, flowers, fountains, sculptures, outdoor benches and cafés, markets and boutiques of the Sparks Street Mall make this a "must see" place to visit. Why not time your visit to coincide with the festival? It will entertain your whole family, from the very youngest to the "very senior" senior.

The Icelandic Festival of Manitoba is a celebration of the Icelandic North Americans' proud tradition and heritage. *Islendingadagurinn*, held each year in Gimli, is one of the oldest ethnic festivals in Canada, its origin dating back to 1890.

Many Icelandic settlers emigrated to Canada after their homes in Iceland were destroyed by volcanic eruptions in 1875. The first festival, in 1890, was the brainchild of Jon Olafsson, editor of the Icelandic newspaper *Logberg*, and the current celebration continues to reflect the interest in Icelandic culture.

Events include theatre programs, musical attractions such as the Gimli Folk Festival, a Tweeners' Dance and a community sing-song. There are also songwriting and poetry competitions.

My friend Mavis, who attends this event each year, tells me that she enjoys the delicious food available in the park. Typical Icelandic foods such as smoked lamb, *skyr* (which is like yogurt), *rullupylsa*, Icelandic brown bread, *hangikjot* and *hardfiskur*, an Icelandic treat of dried cod, are served by participants dressed in Native Icelandic costumes.

Mavis also enjoys taking her grandchildren to the parade on Monday morning, which is filled with clowns, bands, floats and "Vikings."

There are also many sporting events including beach volleyball, a ten-mile run, a tug of war, and the Siglavik Canoe Races. The highlight of the sports events is *Islendingadunk*, the "Viking Challenge." Two contestants sit on a wooden pole stretched across water, and smack each other with pillows until one of them falls in.

The event is attended by Icelandic-Canadians and friends from all across Canada.

The words inscribed on the tombstone of American civil rights leader Dr. Martin Luther King express the focal point of Emancipation Day.

Free at last, free at last, thank God almighty, I'm free at last.

In southern Ontario, a celebration for the freedom of black slaves who came here on the "underground railway" was held as early as 1814. When slavery was abolished in the British Empire in 1834, Emancipation Day became an annual celebration.

On August 1, 1835, St. Catharines, Ontario, became the site of the first official Emancipation Day celebration. Many other southern Ontario towns and cities were soon to follow.

Areas of early black settlements, such as Chatham, Dresden and Wallaceburg, have had (or still have) celebrations that include picnics, parades, services of thanksgiving and fireworks displays.

More recently, the name has been changed to the "Festival of Freedom," and in Amherstburg, near Windsor, the festival draws an enormous crowd.

On August 2nd, Macedonian-Canadians not only honour the prophet Elijah (St. Elijah Day), but they also remember the anniversary of the unsuccessful uprising against the Ottoman Empire. In Toronto, speeches and a huge picnic mark the occasion, which is widely supported by the Macedonian-Canadians in the area.

A religious ceremony of significance takes place on August 6th (or on August 19th in the Eastern churches using the Julian calendar). The Feast of the Transfiguration is observed on this day.

As told in the first three Gospels, Jesus took his three closest disciples, Peter, James and John, to a mountaintop to pray. While he was praying, Jesus appeared to glow and Moses and Elijah seemed to materialize beside him. The disciples were awestruck and fell to the ground. When they raised their heads, they saw only Jesus.

Today, the ceremony is much like a Thanksgiving celebration. In fact, people of Ukrainian background take fruits and flowers to church to be blessed on this day.

August 6, 1945 is a day that will never be forgotten. On this day, Harry S. Truman, president of the United States, announced the bombing of Hiroshima,

July - Canada Day
In 1864, representatives from New
Brunswick, Nova Scotia, Quebec and
Ontario met in Charlottetown, Prince
Edward Island, to consider confederation.
After some three years of discussion
and compromises, it
became a reality.

August - Rakshabandhan
Rakshabandhan is a Hindu festival based
on ancient legend, which honours the ties
between brothers and sisters.

*September - International Day
of Peace*
In 1981, the General Assembly of the
United Nations named its opening day the
"International Day of Peace."

July - Canada Day

August - Rakshabandhan

September - International Day of Peace

Japan, saying "The force from which the sun draws its power has been loosed against those who brought war to the Far East."

The immediate death toll was 60,000, and more than four square miles of the city were wiped out. Three days later, a second atomic bomb was dropped on Nagasaki. It was hoped that the use of a nuclear bomb would bring an end to the war, and indeed, on August 15th Japan surrendered, ending World War II.

However, the problems of radioactive contamination and illness that resulted from the use of this incredibly destructive weapon remain with us even today.

Hiroshima Day is observed in many countries around the world with candlelight vigils and peace marches.

At the Peace Memorial Park in Hiroshima, the ceremony is held in the evening. Thousands of lighted lanterns are set adrift on the Ota River and prayers are offered for world peace.

To my grandchildren and great-grandchildren, for whom World War II is an old movie or a few pages in their history books, I have given the book *Sadako and the Thousand Paper Cranes* by Eleanor Coerr. This book is a beautiful telling of an incredible story. Little Sadako Sasaki was just two years old when the bomb was dropped on Hiroshima. Although it seemed that she had suffered no ill effects from the bomb, ten years later she developed leukemia. While in the hospital, her friend brought in a square of gold paper which Sadako folded into a paper crane. According to legend, if a person who is ill folds one thousand paper cranes, the gods will grant a wish and make him or her well again.

Over the next few months, Sadako folded cranes until she became too ill even to fold paper. At the time of her death, she had folded 644 cranes.

Sadako's classmates folded 356 cranes, so that Sadako was buried with one thousand cranes.

After her passing, her friends at school collected her letters and published them in a book called *Kokeshi*, named for the doll they had given to Sadako while she was in the hospital. Her story spread quickly.

Her friends hoped to build a monument to Sadako and all the children who died as a result of the atomic bomb explosion in Hiroshima. Young people from all over Japan helped to collect money for the project. In 1958, the children's monument was unveiled in the Peace Park in Hiroshima.

Sadako stands on top of a granite mountain of paradise, holding a golden crane in outstretched hands. A Folded Crane Club was organized in her honour, and members still place thousands of origami cranes at the base of the memorial every August.

This is our cry,

This is our prayer;

Peace in the world.

Hindu families have a very lovely celebration in August. *Rakshabandhan* is a festival based on an ancient legend that honours the ties between brothers and sisters.

As the story goes, the god Indram's wife tied a silk charm around his wrist in order to protect him from demons. With this safeguard, Indra was able to defeat his enemies and return to his home in the heavens.

Today, girls tie bracelets called *rakhi*, made of colourful silk or cotton thread, on their brothers' wrists. They also mark their foreheads with coloured vermilion.

The bracelets, symbolizing the bond between brothers and sisters, are usually red, gold or other bright colours mixed with tinsel. When tied on the wrist by his sister, the *rakhi* obliges the brother to protect her. In return for this honour, the brother gives his sister a gift such as clothing, jewellery or money.

Young men who are not lucky enough to have a sister may be selected by a friend to wear a *rakhi*. He will then protect the girl as he would a sister.

Amber Tah, a young neighbour, was happy to tell me of her Rakshabandhan celebration. Amber has a bracelet to give to each of her brothers, and, with the bracelet, she gives each a sweet. Her brothers, in turn, give her a gift, sometimes jewellery, sometimes money, or—Amber's favourite—coupons for a fast food restaurant.

After Amber ties the bracelets on their wrists, she dips uncooked rice in vermilion paint and marks their foreheads.

Many members of Amber's family remain in India, so some weeks before Rakshabandhan, Amber mails *rakhi* to her "cousin-brothers" so that they may be honoured by their Canadian "cousin-sister."

Amber and her family continue to honour this beautiful tradition that began so long ago and so far away.

Acadian Day is probably a misnomer, in that most of the festivals and celebrations honouring the heritage of these French colonial descendants actually last two or three or even ten days!

The Maritime provinces, the original Acadia, hold many local celebrations during the summer months. The largest is the "Acadian Festival" (or *l'Acadia en fête*) in Caraquet, New Brunswick, which includes dance performances, cabaret and concerts, and many sporting events. On the Sunday nearest August 15th, there is an annual blessing of the fleet in the Caraquet harbour. The boats are blessed by a priest as they sail past the main dock.

The actual date of Acadian Day is August 15th, the feast day of Our Lady of Assumption, considered to be the patron saint of Acadia. At six p.m. on this day, Acadians participate in the *Tintamarre*, a cacophony made by drums, whistles and the banging of pots, pans and metal garbage cans.

The Assumption of Mary, on August 15th, is a religious holiday of significance for numerous Catholic congregations. Canadians from many countries celebrate: Greeks, Spaniards, Portugese, Italians and Sicilians are just a few of the celebrants.

The use of the Julian Calendar makes August 28th the day of Assumption for some others. Armenians and Ukrainians also celebrate with a blessing of fruits and flowers on this day.

Members of the Hindu faith celebrate two separate events in August. *Janmashtami* is the festival celebrating the birthday of Lord Krishna, while *Ganesh Chathurthi* is the festival to worship Ganesh, the elephant-headed god of wisdom and success.

May I always have a friendly feeling towards all living beings of the world and may the stream of compassion always flow from my heart towards distressed and afflicted living things.

Jain prayer

Jainism, like Hinduism and Buddhism, originated in India many thousands of years ago. By following traditional Jain teachings, a Jain aspires to *moksha*, perfect liberation from the inner enemies of anger, ego, deceit, etc.

In August or September, Jains observe *Paryushana-parva*, an eight-day religious festival dedicated to introspection, confession and penance. As with most Jain festivals, the Paryushana-parva is a time to focus on the ten cardinal virtues: charity, forgiveness, simplicity, contentment, truthfulness, self-restraint, fasting, detachment, humility and continence. Every Jain asks forgiveness from those whom they have offended during the year, and friendships are restored.

Samvatsari, the last day of the festival, is considered to be the holiest day of the Jain year. It is a day of fasting, meditation, prayer and confession.

People all across Canada love to take advantage of our beautiful summer weather. From coast to coast, there are festivals and celebrations of all types to enjoy.

You may have heard of the Fergus Scottish Festival and Bell's Highland Games, a traditional highland games which includes "heavy events" (such as the caber toss or stone throw), pipe band and highland dance competitions, and Celtic music.

One of my favourites is the Canadian Championship Fiddler's Contest, held in Shelburne, Ontario. For many years, George and I would visit with our close friends, Ray and Elaine Picard, who lived in Shelburne. We would arrive early in the day on Friday and, while George and Ray would enjoy a cup of coffee and a chat, Elaine and I would put together a huge picnic basket filled with our favourite foods: fried chicken, potato salad, coleslaw and Elaine's famous butter tarts.

A Thermos of icy lemonade packed in and we were ready!

The playdowns ran all afternoon and into the evening and the toe-tapping, finger-snapping music never disappointed.

The real fun started later in the evening, however, when we visited the nearby campgrounds. Most of the competitors stayed there in tents or trailers, and groups would get together around big campfires and play their fiddles long into the night. It is a wondrous sight to see youngsters standing beside grandparents and playing their instruments with such joy and enthusiasm. The Fiddler's Contests have some wonderful memories for me.

Food also plays an important role in many summer festivals. From the Peach Festival in Penticton, B.C., the Northern Pike Festival and fish fry in Nipawin, Saskatchewan, and the Shediac Lobster Festival in New Brunswick, to the Labrador Straits Bakeapple Folk Festival, all have one thing in common: delicious food and a chance to enjoy family activities and the camaraderie of friends and neighbours across this great country of ours.

September

September has always been a month that I enjoy. The heavy heat of the summer is past but the chill of autumn has not arrived. I hope you enjoy these lines, from "September" by H. B. Anderson, as much as I do.

A solemn hush broods o'er the peaceful land,
The birds flit, voiceless in the changing trees,
The sumach lights its torch on every hand,
The goldenrod nods in the quiet breeze,
A hint of frost, when sinks the sun to rest;
A mist of white when breaks the dawn of day;
And in the whisper of the mild southwest
We catch the word that Summer's passed away.

The Labour Day weekend is the last long weekend of the summer season.

In North Buxton, Ontario, this weekend is a homecoming for former residents, friends and descendants of the original inhabitants of the town.

Founded originally in 1849, North Buxton became the new home to black slaves who came to

Canada on the "underground railway." Many of the people presently living there are direct descendants of the original settlers.

The homecoming offers us as many as 2,500 visitors to the town to enjoy parties, a dance, a parade and a baseball game.

There is a celebration of a very different type in the Gold Rush city of Dawson, in the Yukon Territory. The Klondike International Outhouse Race has taken place annually on this Labour Day weekend since 1977.

The race, which is taken quite seriously by some athletes, involves four-person teams, each pulling an outhouse on wheels. Many of the competitors wear outrageous costumes and equip their outhouses with such modern-day luxuries as carpeted seats and cellular phones. At the end of the three-kilometre race there are awards for the best-dressed racers as well as the "fastest outhouse." The Grand Trophy is a wooden outhouse with an engraved plaque.

The Labour Day holiday falls on the first Monday in September. More than 100 years ago, workers in Canada, particularly new immigrants, worked in dreadful conditions for ridiculously low wages. Unions were desperately needed to protect the workers' rights, but at that time, unions were illegal.

In 1872, as a result of a city-wide printer's strike in Toronto, the federal government passed legislation that gave official recognition to the trade union movement.

The unions wanted their political strength and solidarity never to be forgotten. They organized annual parades and, in 1888, petitioned the federal government for a national day to be known as Labour Day. Finally, in 1894, it was declared by an act of parliament that the first Monday in September would be Labour Day and that it would be celebrated as a national holiday.

Unions hold parades in many cities across the country, one of the largest being in Toronto, where the parade marches into the Canadian National Exhibition grounds on the final day of the C.N.E.

Established in 1966 by the United Nations to encourage universal literacy, International Literacy Day has been observed on September 8th by all countries and organizations that are part of the United Nations.

This day holds particular interest for me. I grew up in a family of voracious readers. Almost nothing in my life has given me more pleasure than reading a good book. My husband and I encouraged this love in our children and grandchildren, and more recently, my daughter Margaret and I have become volunteers in our local school, helping children learn to read and write.

The gateway to all knowledge is understanding and literacy. How important it is for us here in our country to encourage literacy—not just with our children, but with each and every citizen.

Many Egyptian-Canadians belong to the Coptic Orthodox Church (the native Christian Church in Egypt). For them, the New Year is celebrated on September 11th. This may seem like a strange time of year to observe the new year, but the rationale for it is very reasonable.

The Dog Star, Sirius, is the brightest star in the sky. The ancient Egyptians calculated their year from the time that Sirius reappeared, after a brief absence from the Egyptian sky, just before dawn on September 11th. This reappearance signalled the flooding of the Nile over the fertile plains area and the beginning of the new planting season. And so it was that September 11th became the Egyptian New Year.

The church, also celebrating the New Year on this day, commemorates the martyrs of the church by having the priests wear red vestments. As well, the altar is covered with a red cloth for the Coptic New Year service. Red dates are particularly significant for worshippers today. The red skin is said to symbolize the blood of the martyrs, the white meat inside represents the purity of their hearts, and the pit depicts their steadfast faith.

In the United States, there is a special day set aside in September called Grandparents Day. Established by President Richard M. Nixon on September 6, 1979, it is a day not of gift giving, but of participation in grandchildren's school classes or special assembly programs.

Although this is not an "official" day in Canada, my grandchildren have often sent greeting cards to commemorate the day.

For me, "Grandparents Day" is every day that I have a chance to be with my grandchildren and great-grandchildren. I have the chance to enjoy their company and listen to their hopes and dreams, without the pressure of being their parent and the responsibilities that it entails. Grandchildren are God's reward for growing old.

Chilean-Canadians commemorate the independence of their country (in 1818) with a *peña*, or party. They sing and dance and enjoy such special food as *empañadas* (meat pastries with an egg and olive filling) and *chicha*, a drink much like cider.

Many Chileans came to Canada after the overthrow of Salvador Allende's Marxist government in 1973. Coincidentally, Allende was elected president on this same date, September 18, 1970.

A *peña* of much larger proportions is held at the C.N.E. grounds in Toronto. Mid-September is the time that many Spanish-speaking countries celebrate their national holidays. Canadians from Costa Rica, El Salvador, Guatemala, Honduras, Nicaragua and Mexico join together for a huge Hispanic Festival. There is so much to enjoy—delicious foods from every children do get an idea of what peace can mean for them.

September 22 or 23 signals the arrival of autumn, the most beautiful season in Canada.

Autumn is a gypsy
With jewels in her hair,

Autumn is a gypsy
Gay and debonair,
Dancing in the sunshine
At the harvest fair,
With confetti whirling
In the golden air.

Autumn is a gypsy
With jewels in her hair.

When the sun crosses the plane of the earth's equator on March 21st and again on September 21st, night and day are of equal length all over the world. This is known as the vernal equinox.

Members of the Wiccan faith celebrate *Mabon* (also called Harvest Home) on September 22nd. Most festivals of the Wiccan church follow the region, music, native dancing and, for the children, *piñatas*.

For some Roman Catholics and members of the Greek Orthodox Church, September 14th marks the Feast of the Exaltation of the Holy Cross. Special church services celebrate the discovery of the cross on which Jesus was crucified. (There is also a holiday on May 3rd, when Filipino groups celebrate Santa Cruzan, or the Day of Commemoration of the Holy Cross.)

In Greece, the priest of the church will throw a cross from the shore into the sea. Many young men dive into the depths until the cross is found. The finder keeps the cross and receives a blessing.

Some churches in Nova Scotia continue that tradition, but in many areas across our country it is too cold even for the hardiest of divers.

In 1981, the General Assembly of the United Nations named its opening day the "International Day of Peace." Since then, many schools across Canada have chosen to have peace assemblies or some other form of commemoration for this day.

At our local school, each class is responsible for making a "Peace Wreath," and these wreaths are presented at a "Peace Assembly," a celebration of music and poetry. At the end of the assembly, all students join hands and sing the beautiful "Let There Be Peace on Earth." It is really very moving and I feel that the logic of seasonal progression, and the festival gives testament to this. Mabon celebrates the encapsulation of life in the form of the seed in which it survives the cold barren winter. Mabon also celebrates the grape harvest or "Harvest of the Vine," which symbolizes the power of the Goddess to change the sweet nectar of youth into the wisdom of old age and spiritual maturity.

Our Chinese-Canadian friends have a Mid-Autumn Festival which falls on the fifteenth day of the eighth month, toward the end of September. This is also known as the "Moon Festival," because it is held at the time of the full moon. Centuries ago, the Babylonians and other ancient peoples compared the moon to a boat, which floats over the ocean of heaven. The Chinese saw more. They saw a hare sitting under a cassia tree: the hare is using the leaves and the bark of the tree to prepare a drug that, supposedly, assures long life.

It was the old custom for the women of the family to build an altar in the courtyard of the house. In the centre of the altar was a long-eared hare and a plate of thirteen moon cakes, one for each month of the Chinese year.

The tasty moon cakes are still made today, and there are twenty to thirty varieties. Their round moon-shape symbolizes family unity. These cakes are made with a greyish flour and are often filled with spices, nuts, lotus seed paste, or red bean paste. Some even have a duck egg in the centre.

The Mid-Autumn Festival is often held outdoors. People usually travel long distances to be together, and family reunions are traditional on this day. Picnics or feasts of crabmeat, fruit and rice cakes are part of the celebration.

Before the feast, there is a lantern procession. The lanterns are often elaborate and very colourful, and their shapes are symbolic of ancient Chinese beliefs. As you would imagine, the most common shape is round (like the moon), symbolizing perfect joy and the cycle of life. Lobster-shaped lanterns will bring happiness and contentment; butterflies signal long life; and the fish assures that the owner will do well scholastically.

Traditionally, this festival comes after the harvest, and it becomes a time to rest and enjoy life.

The Mid-Autumn Festival is celebrated by many Asian communities. In Korea it is called *Hangwai* or *Ch'usok*; in Hong Kong it is *Chung Ch'iu*; and in Taiwan, it is called *Tiong-chhiu Choeh*.

In Vietnam, the Mid-Autumn Festival is a children's day, known as *Trung-Thu*. The children carry lanterns, shaped like fish, dragons or boats, in the Lion Parade. Here in Canada, Vietnamese celebrations are similar, complete with a lion parade and lantern processions.

Corn, beans and squash are all vegetables indigenous to North America, and they were first cultivated by Native North Americans. Before the beginning of the corn harvest, when the corn is still green in the husks, the Iroquois hold three days of religious ceremonies, known as the "Green Corn Festival," to give thanks to the Creator for the bountiful harvest. Sacred dances, storytelling and prayers are all part of this traditional celebration.

Many years ago, it was the custom for the Iroquois to build a small ceremonial council fire. One by one, those participating in the sacred ritual of thanksgiving moved toward the flames, sprinkled dried tobacco leaves on the fire and raised their faces and hands to the sky while murmuring sacred words.

Today, the Great Feather Dance, The Skin Dance of Thanksgiving, and the sacred Peachstone betting game are all a part of the three-day festival. There is a Harvest Ceremony, a one-day celebration held at the end of the corn harvest.

Long ago, Iroquoian women gathered the corn, which was roasted or boiled while green; parched and pounded into meal when dry. Iroquois families ate mush, hominy and corn dumplings. Corn soup, succotash and popcorn were also a part of their diet. From dried husks, they made moccasins, masks and dolls. Corncob fires, nearly smokeless, warmed their teepees and lodges.

Corn is one of the world's greatest bounties, and we can thank our First Canadians for this delicious vegetable, an important part of our autumn harvest.

We return thanks to the corn, and to her sisters, the beans and the squashes, which give us life.

From a prayer of Thanksgiving

Growing naturally in the bountiful marshland and shallow lakes of Ontario, Manitoba, and Saskatchewan, wild rice, the "food of the North," is a traditional staple food of the Algonkians, Northern Cree and Ojibwa.

The wild rice harvest in fall is a family event for Native Canadian families. Harvesting techniques have changed very little in a thousand years.

Families often returned to the same location every year, and each clan had its own share of the harvest. Ojibwa women would braid rice stalks together along the borders to mark out the area of harvest for each family.

When the rice grains are hard they are ready to harvest. Wild rice is gathered from a canoe. One person poles the canoe through the marsh while another person, seated in the stern of the canoe, bends down the stalks with one stick and, using a second stick, knocks off the rice kernels into the bottom of the canoe. When the canoe is full of rice they return to shore.

The rice is spread out to dry and then parched to loosen the husks. To remove the husks the rice is pounded with long wooden sticks. The rice is then "winnowed," or tossed in the air so that the light-weight husks blow away and the rice falls into a tray. The rice can then be stored in bags.

Wild rice is a favourite accompaniment for game or wild fowl. This recipe for Pine Nut Wild Rice has the delicious nutty flavour of wild rice and can be served with a variety of different meats or fowl. I particularly enjoy it with roast duck.

Pine Nut Wild Rice

1/2 cup wild rice, uncooked

2 tbsp. green onions/tops, sliced

1 tsp. margarine or butter

1 1/2 cups chicken broth

2 oz. pine nuts, toasted

1/2 cup pears, dried and chopped

1/2 cup currants

1. Cook and stir wild rice and onions in margarine in a two-quart heavy saucepan over medium heat until onions are tender, about 3 minutes.

2. Stir in broth. Heat to boiling, stirring occasionally. Reduce heat and cover. Simmer until wild rice is tender, about 40 to 50 minutes.

3. Stir in pine nuts, pears and currants.

In late September or early October, our Jewish friends celebrate the most important festivals of their religious year. *Rosh Hashanah*, the Jewish New Year, is observed on the first and second days of *Tishri*, the seventh month of the Jewish year. *Yom Kippur*, the Day of Atonement, falls on the tenth day of the month. The Jewish High Holy Days, or *Yamim Nora'im*, are observed during the ten-day period between Rosh Hashanah and Yom Kippur. Known as the Days of Awe or the Days of Repentance, it is a time of reflection and self examination, a time to ask God for forgiveness of sins. It is also a time to forgive others so that the new year may begin in harmony.

Rosh Hashanah is the two-day Jewish New Year celebration. On these days people greet each other with the words *Le shanah tovah*, "For a good year," which is short for the traditional greeting of the day "May God write you down for a good year in the Book of Life."

In synagogues across the country the day begins with the blowing of the *shofar*, or ram's horn, which serves as a reminder that although Abraham was willing to obey God's command and sacrifice his son Isaac, God allowed him to sacrifice a lamb instead. The *shofar*, which is very difficult to play, makes a unique, wailing sound and is a call to penitence.

At home the family usually celebrates the New Year with a festive dinner. The menu may vary from home to home according to taste, but on every table you will find honey and fresh fruit. The honey is "for a sweet year," and the fruit represents ancient times when Rosh Hashanah was also a harvest festival. The first night's meal begins with apple dipped in honey. *Challah*, or egg bread, is baked in a circle instead of being braided as usual. The round *challah* symbolizes the continuity of life and a wish for a year without unhappiness or sorrow. It is also dipped in honey before it is eaten.

Yom Kippur, known as the Day of Atonement, is the holiest and most solemn day of the Jewish year. It is a strict day of fasting; not even water may be taken from sundown to sundown. Many adults spend the day in prayer in the synagogue where they will confess their sins then make atonement to God to obtain his forgiveness. The day comes to a close with a long blast on the *shofar* and the words "Hear, O Israel, the Lord our God, the Lord is One," and then "Next Year in Jerusalem."

September 29th is Michaelmas, sometimes known as St. Michael and All Angels. Regarded as the greatest host of angels, St. Michael is honoured in the Roman Catholic, Anglican and Orthodox churches.

In England it was once the custom to eat roast goose on Michaelmas. When tenants paid their rent on this day they often included "one goose fit for the Lord's dinner." It is still the custom to enjoy a goose dinner in Ireland.

There is an old saying that if you eat goose on Michaelmas you won't have to worry about money for a year. I remember my mother telling me this and I also recall our family eating goose on this day. We must have been the exception to this rule (or perhaps it didn't apply to our family)!

October

Now the wild geese are going over,
Clanking their chains on the windless sky,
Over the cornfields, over the clover,
Shouting their wild exuberant cry:
"Come with us, come with us—come"

They are calling,
And I, with no answer shaped in my mouth,
Stand where the painted leaves are falling,
Watching them disappear in the south,

Disappear from my sight and hearing,
Going to who knows what far land,
Straight as an arrow, and not fearing
The journey ahead...

I lift my hand
Bidding them to stay their avid going
Across the wide and uncharted track,
Calling to them, and yet well knowing
That only the spring will bring them back.

This poem, "Autumn Flight" by Grace Noll Crowell,
could well have been written from the Ontario town of
Kingsville. Located on Lake Ontario, just southeast of
Windsor, it is the site of Jack Miner's Bird Sanctuary,

and for decades it has been welcoming the migrating Canada geese as they head for warmer climes. The Migration Festival at the sanctuary happens around mid-October, depending upon the arrival time of the geese, which of course depends upon the weather.

Just a few miles further east of Kingsville, at Point Pelee, butterfly watchers gather in October to see the migrating monarch butterflies. This event may soon be a thing of the past, however, as the monarchs have so diminished in numbers that they have become an endangered species.

Until a few hundred years ago most people had only the food they produced for themselves. It is no surprise then, that the harvest was so important, and that when the grain had been harvested, the hay stored in the barns and the fruits and vegetables canned or stored in cold cellars, it was time to have the harvest festival.

When the last sheaf was picked up it was hoisted high and the "harvest shout" was raised.

Well ploughed!
Well sowed!
Well harrowed!
Well mowed!
And all safely carted to the barn
With never a load throwed!
Hip, hip, hooray!

October - Thanksgiving
In early October, when the harvest is
complete, families pause to
give thanks for all the good things
given to them.

November - Remembrance Day
To honour the memory of the soldiers who
died defending our country, we observe a
two-minute silence at 11 a.m., the hour at
which the hostilities ended.

December - Hanukkah
Hanukkah is a Jewish celebration that
takes place around the time of the winter
solstice and lasts for eight days.

October - Thanksgiving

In Flanders fields
the poppies blow

Lest we forget

November - Remembrance Day

December - Hanukkah

Although machinery such as combine harvesters have taken over much of the work it is still the custom to get together for a harvest festival or fall fair to sample what has been produced.

In western Canada, "Threshermen's Days" are popular harvest time festivals, with importance placed on contests of farming skills such as grain threshing.

The Welland Canal, linking Lake Erie and Lake Ontario, flows between vineyards thick with grapes. To climax the harvest, the city of St. Catharines welcomes visitors to the Niagara Grape and Wine Festival. My good friend and former neighbour Enid Darroch has a daughter, Gail Benjafield, living in St. Catharines. Gail, a librarian and local historian, was a most gracious hostess and "tour guide" for my visit to this popular festival.

We enjoyed a barbecue, several gourmet wine-tasting events, a street dance (which I watched), and the crowning of the Grape King and Queen of the festival.

I particularly enjoyed the Pied Piper Parade, an enormously entertaining parade of children who were dressed in a variety of funny or fancy costumes.

If you are in the area near the end of September this is a festival well worth taking time to enjoy.

Another festival of a different type takes place in Kleinburg, Ontario. The Binder Twine Festival began in 1891, the result of an interesting problem.

Farmers in the area used binder twine to tie together their sheaves of grain. Local tinsmith Charlie Shaw was the supplier of the twine, but a problem had developed. For some reason mice liked to eat the twine. So that the farmers could get "uneaten" twine, Charlie asked that all of the farmers come to town to collect the twine shipment on the day that it arrived by train.

For some of the farmers it became a time to visit with friends and neighbours, and soon it became an annual social gathering. When Mr. Shaw died in the 1930s the event ended. However, it was revived in 1967 as a Centennial project and it has been a popular festival each year since then.

People who live by the sea enjoy a harvest of a different type. The fishing season, which usually ends in October, provides us with an abundance of various types of fish and delicacies such as lobster, shrimp, and scallops. In places such as Lunenburg, Nova Scotia, there is a Fisheries Exhibition and Reunion. At Christian harvest festivals at churches in fishing ports, freshly caught fish and fish nets are often displayed with flowers, fruits, and vegetables. A favourite hymn for this time of year is the Manx Fishermen's Hymn:

Our wives and children we commend to Thee;
For them we plough the land and plough the deep;
For them by day the golden corn we reap,
By night the silver harvest of the sea.

Canada boasts a variety of apple types, most of which are ripe in the autumn. In many areas from British Columbia to Nova Scotia, Apple Festivals are annual fall events. Apple butter, apple fritters, apple syrup and good old-fashioned apple pie are just some of the ways to enjoy this delicious fruit.

In Mennonite communities it is still the practice to hold *schnitzing* bees, where families and friends get together to peel, core and slice the apples to "schnitz," or make dried apple rings.

On October 4th, the feast of St. Francis commemorates the saint's transition from this life to the afterlife. For two days, the town of Assisi, Italy, is lit up by oil lamps burning consecrated oil.

St. Francis believed that all created things belong to God. He felt a kinship to all creatures, people, animals and birds and his gentle curiosity and kindness made him beloved by all.

To honour St. Francis, many churches hold a ceremony of blessing animals. Boys and girls are invited to bring their pets to the church to be blessed, and this ceremony becomes more popular each year.

The festival of *Sukkot* begins the fifth day after Yom Kippur on the fifteenth day of *Tishri*. The Sukkot festival makes quite a drastic transition from one of the most solemn holidays to one of the most joyous. The seven-day festival is sometimes called *Zeman Simkhateinu*, the Season of Our Rejoicing. The two days following the festival are separate holidays, *Shemini Atzeret* and *Simkhat Torah*, but are commonly thought of as part of Sukkot.

The name of the festival comes from the practice of building little booths (*sukkah*) in the fields during harvest, and from the temporary dwellings in which the Israelites lived as they wandered in the desert for forty years after their departure from Egypt.

The traditional way of observing Sukkot is to build a small booth or tabernacle and live in it during the nine days. These small huts usually have three walls and a roof covered with material that will not blow away in the wind. They are decorated with flowers, fruit and leafy branches.

Jewish families in Canada often eat all of their meals in the sukkah. Nowadays, Orthodox congregations build a sukkah in the synagogue, while some Reform Jews choose to make miniature models of the ancient huts and use them as centrepieces on the family's dinner table.

Special prayers of joy are said in the synagogue and in the sukkah. Another observance that is a part of the services involves what are known as The Four Species. A palm branch, three myrtle twigs and two willow branches are bound together and are collectively called the *lulav*, held in the right hand. An *etrog* (a large citrus fruit) is held in the left hand. With these four species in hand, one recites a blessing and waves in all directions to "rejoice before the Lord" and to symbolize God's universality.

On the seventh day of Sukkot, known as *Hoshanah Rabbah*, these symbolic plants are used again. Carrying the Four Species, seven circuits are made around the *bimah* (the pedestal where the Torah is read). These processions are known as Hoshanahs because a prayer with the refrain *"Hosha na"* ("Please save us!") is recited.

During *Shemini Atzeret*, on the eighth day Jews pray for rain and on the ninth day, *Simhat Torah*, or "Rejoicing for the Law" marks the completion and new beginning of the annual cycle of the reading of the Torah in synagogue.

Festivals of thanks for a bountiful harvest are probably as old as farming itself.

Here in North America it is generally thought that the original Thanksgiving Day dates back to 1621 in Plymouth Colony, where the Pilgrims joined with Massasoit, chief of the Wampanoag tribe, and about ninety of his tribesmen in a three-day feast. In fact, fifty-three years before the Pilgrims' celebration, Sir Martin Frobisher and the English settlers in the area held a harvest celebration of thanksgiving in what is now Newfoundland.

For flowers that bloom about our feet;
For tender grass so fresh and sweet;
For song of bird and hum of bee;
For all things fair we hear and see,
Father in Heaven we thank Thee.

Ralph Waldo Emerson

Early October, when harvest is complete, has been the time when families paused to give thanks for all the good things given to us. Although each family celebrates in its own way, generally speaking this is the most family-oriented holiday next to Christmas. Family is usually one of the most important parts of our lives and something to be grateful for.

Our family is no exception. Although we are widely scattered, nearly all of our family members make a great effort to attend the family get-together.

Sunday of this weekend is a time of celebration in Christian churches. At this service we thank God for the "fruits of the earth in their season and for the labour of those who harvest them."

Our family always enjoys a traditional turkey dinner that includes roast turkey with wild rice and sausage stuffing, mashed potatoes, turnip, and pumpkin pie for dessert.

It's interesting to know that pumpkins and other members of the squash family are indigenous to the New World. Early settlers from Europe had never seen these plants, but when the plants transported from Europe failed to thrive in the harsh Canadian climates, the settlers were happy to find out about these new edible fruits and vegetables.

There are many recipes for pumpkin pie, but this is a particular favourite of mine.

Pumpkin Pie

2 tbsp. all-purpose flour

1/2 tsp. each of salt, ginger, mace, nutmeg, cinnamon

1/3 cup brown sugar

1/4 cup maple syrup

1 cup scalded milk

2 eggs, well beaten

1 1/2 cups canned pumpkin

10-inch unbaked pie shell

Whipped cream (optional)

1. Mix all the ingredients together (except whipped cream).
2. Pour mixture into the unbaked pie shell.
3. Bake in a hot 450° F oven for 10 minutes; reduce heat to 325° F and bake 30 to 40 minutes longer or until the filling is firm. (A knife inserted in the centre should come out clean.)
4. Cool before serving. Serve with whipped cream if desired.

We here in Canada have so much to be thankful for. We have many freedoms that we take for granted—free speech, freedom of religion and worship, the freedom to choose our government and our destiny. These are all important parts of the democracy that is our heritage.

Friends in the Baha'i faith celebrate the anniversary of the birth of Bab, herald of the new age for Baha'is.

The Bab, the Exalted One,

Is the Morn of Truth,

The splendour of Whose light

Shineth throughout all regions.

He is also the Harbinger of

The Most Great Light.

Abdu'l-Baha

October sees a special celebration in the Buddhist faith as well. Founder's Day on October 16th commemorates the formal introduction of Buddhism into Canada in 1905, and the first assembly of Buddhists in Toronto in 1980.

When Christopher Columbus convinced King Ferdinand and Queen Isabella to finance his plan to find a route to the Orient by sailing west, he guessed that he needed to sail only about 2,400 miles. So it was that when he landed in the Bahamas he believed that he had arrived in the East Indies. Although he was incorrect, he is credited with opening the New World to colonization.

In the United States October 12th is called Columbus Day and it is observed on the second Monday in October. Fifth Avenue in New York City is the setting for a huge parade, now a tradition.

In many Latin American countries this day is *Dia de la Raza*, Day of the Race. Here in Canada, Dia de la Raza is a time to enjoy a dinner-dance, parties and cultural programs.

There are a number of Hindu festivals that celebrate the victory of good and evil. *Navaratri*, meaning nine nights, is the longest Hindu festival.

In eastern India the festival is known as *Durga Puja*, honouring the goddess Durga, the personification of energy. Durga has nine incarnations, so Hindus pray to her in nine different forms in order to receive her full power.

In the states of southern India, the festival is known as *Navaratri*, and herein the goddesses Lakshmi and Sarasvati are worshipped. Lakshmi is associated with wealth and good luck while Sarasvati is linked to fertility, wisdom and education.

In Nepal the festival is known as *Dasain*, and Buddhists join in the celebration with special events held in the Buddhist shrines. On the first day of the festival a *kalash* (water jug) is filled with holy water, and barley seeds are planted in a dish of cow dung. During the festival the seeds are sprinkled with the water and special prayers are said in front of the water until *Dussehra* (the tenth day after Navaratri) starts. Children receive blessings from their elders, and to symbolize this each child is given a red *tika* (dot) on the forehead and a new shoot of barley.

In Canada the nine-day festival is often shortened to three days, starting on the seventh day of the new moon. There is a feast and, as in Holi, people visit from house to house, sharing sweets at each place that they visit.

Dussehra, the tenth night, celebrates the victory of Lord Rama over Ravana. The story is told in the epic poem "Ramayana." Lord Rama woos and wines the beautiful Sita, whom he marries. She is carried off by the evil ten-headed Ravana, demon king of Lanka. Rama slays Ravana and the forces of good prevail over evil.

In Canadian temples it is customary to read the Ramayana in twenty-four hours. After its completion everyone joins in the celebration by eating sweets and watching fireworks.

Halloween is one of the very oldest holidays, tracing its origins back thousands of years. The holiday we know as Halloween has had a multitude of influences from many cultures.

The ultimate origins come from the ancient Celtic harvest festival, *Samhain*, a time when people believed that the spirits of the dead roamed the earth. The Samhain festival usually lasted three days and many people would parade in costumes made from animal skins.

When the Romans invaded Britain in the first century, Pomona Day, named for the goddess of fruits and gardens, was celebrated around November 1st.

With the spread of Christianity, November 1st was named All Saints' Day. November 2nd, All Souls' Day, honoured the dead with bonfires, parades and people dressing in costumes as saints, angels and devils.

The Halloween that is celebrated today is a combination of all of these influences: Pomona Day's apples, nuts and harvest treats; Sanhain's black cats, magic, evil spirits and death; and the ghosts, skeletons and skulls from All Saints' Day and All Souls' Day.

The original "jack-o-lanterns" were carved by the Celts out of big turnips. When the early settlers came to America, they found that the pumpkin was larger and more colourful than the turnip. It soon replaced the turnip as the jack-o-lantern and became the most widely recognized symbol of Halloween.

On Halloween night, the children of the neighbourhood come trick-or-treating. This practice goes back to the early celebration of All Souls' Day. The poor would go begging and the homeowners would give them a special treat, a soul cake.

Halloween is a day that I really enjoy. I have so many fond memories of making costumes for my daughters. Although I could never be called a seamstress I did have a happy knack for putting together imaginative costumes. I always look forward with happy anticipation the little costumed callers that come begging "Trick or Treat."

From ghoulies and ghosties and
Long-leggedy beasties
And things that go bump in the night,
Good Lord, deliver us!

November

There is a lovely prayer for the November 1st celebration of All Saints' Day.

We thank Thee, O God, for the saints of all ages; for those who, in times of darkness, kept the lamp of faith burning; for the great souls who saw visions of large truth and dared to declare it; for the multitude of quiet and gracious souls whose presence has purified and sanctified the world; and for those known and loved by us who have passed from this earthly fellowship into the fuller light of life with Thee. Amen.

Many Protestant churches and also those of the Roman Catholic and Anglican faith keep November 1st as a celebration of all the Christian saints—most particularly for those who have no special feast days of their own.

This day is sometimes known as All Hallomas or All Hallow's Day, and the idea for the celebration goes back to the fourth century. At that time Greek Christians observed a festival on the first Sunday after Pentecost, in late May or early June, to honour all saints and martyrs.

In the seventh century, Pope Boniface IV dedicated the Pantheon to the Virgin and all the martyrs. The date of celebration was May 1st.

It is thought that moving the day to November 1st was an attempt to replace the pagan festival *Samhain*.

In the Middle Ages, so few people could read or write that it was common practice to mark Sundays and other special days on the calendar with red ink. These holidays came to be known as "red letter days."

My husband George used to say that All Saints' Day was a good time for us to pause, remember and give thanks for all those good people who make our lives a little better. A patient school teacher, a friend with whom we can share our joys and our sorrows, a neighbour's child who mows our lawn; all are "saints" who touch our lives and give it meaning and worth.

Some years after the Roman Catholic Church named November 1st All Saints' Day, St. Odilo, the Abbot of Cluny in France, proposed that the day after All Saints' Day be set aside in honour of the departed. All Souls' Day was primarily a Catholic, Anglican and Orthodox holy day until the end of the First World War. Faced with the crushing loss of so many young people, it was decided by the Protestant churches that they would pray for the souls of all those lost and set All Souls' Day as a holy day.

In many Catholic countries it is the custom to visit family graves to honour ancestors. In England children used to go from house to house where they were given "soul cakes" and a bit of fruit. The soul cake was supposed to rescue souls from purgatory, and apples were thought to give immortality.

A soul! A soul! A soul cake!

Please, good Missus, a soul cake!

An apple, a pear, a plum or a cherry,

Any good thing to make us all merry,

One for Peter, two for Paul,

Three for Him who made us all!

A traditional English song

Dia Dos Finados, the Portugese celebration for this day, is observed with special Masses and visitations to cemeteries to take flowers and pay respects to departed relatives.

Il Giorno dei Morti, All Souls' Day for Italians, begins with a solemn Mass, the Requiem for the dead. Graves of family members are decorated with flowers and candles. This is very similar to the Polish All Souls' Day, *Ozien Zaduszny*. They, too, remember their departed relatives with flowers and vigil lights on the graves.

On November 4, 1605, thirty-six barrels of gunpowder were found in the basement of the Houses of Parliament in London, England. Upset by the persecution of Roman Catholics, the conspirators of the "Gunpowder Plot" planned to blow up King James I and his government. Someone tipped off the King's ministers and Guy Fawkes, along with a number of other men, was discovered and arrested. On January 31st, eight of the conspirators were executed and a grateful Parliament established November 5th as a national day of thanksgiving.

To celebrate the defeat many people burned Guy Fawkes in effigy. It became common practice for children to collect old clothes and trash to make the effigy figure, and they would ask for a "penny for the guy," which they would spend on fireworks.

Although Guy Fawkes didn't originate the plan to blow up the king, the day of thanksgiving was known as Guy Fawkes Day.

On the night of November 5th it is still a common sight in Britain to see grand bonfires and fireworks filling the sky in remembrance of the failed Gunpowder Plot.

Here in Canada, English and Irish immigrants in Newfoundland continue the tradition of lighting bonfires. All along the coast in small towns and villages giant bonfires light up the sky, and often it becomes quite competitive to see whose fire can be seen from the greatest distance. In Newfoundland, November 5th is known as Bonfire Night, although on occasion an effigy figure of "the guy" will be tossed into the flames.

Immigrants from the West Indies are also familiar with Bonfire Night, as it is a celebration of some fun and fireworks there as well.

The so-called Gunpowder Plot has given rise to a most interesting tradition in England. In early November, members of parliament return, after the long summer recess, to the State Opening of Parliament, a colourful ritual. Her Majesty the Queen arrives in a horse-drawn coach dressed in the robes of state, and she reads a speech written by members of the government outlining plans for the coming session.

Before the members of parliament or the Queen arrive, the basements of both houses are searched, a traditional part of the opening ceremony.

How many of you can remember a silly celebration called Sadie Hawkins Day? Al Capp, a cartoonist, invented the homely Sadie Hawkins and her day in his cartoon strip in the 1930s. On the first Saturday in November, spinsters could chase bachelors and, if caught, the men were obligated to marry the women who trapped them. For decades the "Sadie Hawkins Dance" in early November was extraordinarily popular. Young ladies invited male friends to the dance and it was obligatory to accept the first invitation received.

I can remember my girls in eager conversations around the dinner table, lining up their "targets" for the Saturday night dance. They would set lofty goals—the quarterback of the football team, the captain of the soccer or lacrosse team, but in the end they would usually ask a neighbour or someone that they already knew well.

"Sadie Hawkins" dances are probably rare now, as it has become quite common practice for the female to ask the male for a date. Ah me, I guess some things have changed forever.

Members of the Baha'i faith celebrate the birth of Baha'u'llah on November 12th. Born as Mirza Husayn-Ali, son of a wealthy merchant, he was an adherent of Islam, and later, a follower of Bab (founder of the Baha'i faith).

In 1863 Husayn-Ali declared himself the messenger of God as foretold by Bab, and he took the name Baha'u'llah, meaning "the glory of God."

Interested in improving the quality of life for all, Baha'u'llah encouraged such progressive ideas as universal education, equality of the sexes and a spirit of friendship and fellowship between people of all races and religions. Members of the Baha'i faith believe that the work of Baha'u'llah will one day unite the world in peace.

> O Friend! In the garden of thy heart plant naught but the rose of love.

> *Baha'u'llah*

The Baha'i faith is growing steadily in Canada. My dear friends Isabelle and Don Weaver are members of the Baha'i community, and their kindness and goodness are an example for all. Both do volunteer work in the local home for the aged, feeding elderly residents or working with the highly popular bingo nights. They are good friends and neighbours and their happy and positive nature brightens this small corner of the world.

Canada has a particularly strong tie to the Baha'i faith, as in 1937 a Montreal woman married the great-grandson of the Bab. Her home—the Maxwell House in Montreal—is a Baha'i pilgrimage site. There is also a National Centre in Thornhill and an Association for Baha'i Studies in Ottawa.

The Sikh religion was founded in the state of Punjab (now Pakistan) in the late fifteenth century. Each year in November, Sikhs around the world celebrate the birth of Guru Nanak, founder of the faith. The holy Sikh scriptures, known as the *Guru Granth Sahib*, are read from beginning to end. The readings take place in the temples over a period of two days and nights ending with a *langar*, a shared meal where everyone must eat a bit of *Karah parshad*, a sweet dessert. It is a time of great joy.

Holocaust Day (*Yom Hashoah*) was a day established by Israel's *Knesset* (parliament) to honour the millions of Jews who died tragically in the

Second World War. It is observed on the twenty-seventh day of the Jewish month of *Nisan* (between April 8 and May 6).

In Toronto, November has been named Holocaust Remembrance Month, and it is hoped that events such as lectures or films and school visits will bring a greater understanding of the horror that was the Holocaust.

At the eleventh hour of the eleventh day of the eleventh month, 1918, the armistice between the Allied and Central Powers was signed that ended the First World War. To honour the memory of the soldiers who died defending our country, we observe a two-minute silence at 11 a.m., the hour at which the hostilities ended.

In 1931 the Canadian Parliament changed the name from Armistice Day to Remembrance Day and made November 11th a legal holiday. After the Second World War ended, Remembrance Day became a day to honour all of the fallen heroes from the two Great Wars.

Although many years have passed since the Second World War ended, there are those of us whose memories of those dark days remain very vivid. As one veteran said, "My work in the Air Force remains, to this day, the most important thing I ever did in my life. I know that the young people who haven't known war may never understand this, but it is enough that I do, and that I can look back with pride and say, 'I made a difference.'"

The Canadian poet John McCrae wrote the poem that has come to symbolize this day. His immortal lines still move me to tears.

In Flanders fields the poppies blow
Between the crosses, row on row,
That mark our place; and in the sky,
The larks, still bravely singing, fly
Scarce heard amid the guns below.

We are the Dead. Short days ago
We lived, felt dawn, saw sunset glow,
Loved and were loved, and now we lie
In Flanders fields.

Take up our quarrel with the foe:
To you from failing hands we throw
The torch; be yours to hold it high,
If ye break faith with us who die
We shall not sleep, tho' poppies grow
In Flanders fields.

Shichi-Go-San (the Seven-Five-Three Festival) is an ancient Japanese celebration that is often one of the first events that a Japanese child will remember. Seven-year-old girls, five-year-old boys, and all three-year-olds are taken to the Shinto shrine where their birth has been recorded and their parents give thanks to the deities for having taken care of them and to ask for further blessings.

At three, a little girl wears her hair dressed for the first time, similar to her mother's. The five-year-old boy will wear his first full kimono, and at seven the girls wear their first *obi*, or wide kimono belt.

After the priest has prayed for their healthy growth he gives two little boxes to each child. One contains cakes in the form of Shinto emblems (mirror, sword and jewel); the other is sacred rice to be mixed with the evening meal. Many parents plan parties for their children on this day, the Sunday nearest to November 15th.

Divali (also called *Diwali* or *Dipanali*) is a most popular Hindu festival. *Divali* means a "row or cluster of lights" and the festival, celebrated by both Hindus and Sikhs, is called the "Feast of Lights."

Clay saucers filled with mustard oil and floating cotton wicks give a soft glowing light. During Divali Hindus in India light thousands of these small lamps (called *divas)* or candles, and these lights are one of India's most spectacular events.

The festival is held at the new moon in late October or early November, when the nights are long and dark. It comes about a month after Navaratri. By tradition Divali lasts about five days, and the festivities are illuminated by the lamps, fireworks and bonfires.

In the Punjab, the third day of the festival is Divali proper, commemorating Lord Rama's return to his Kingdom with his wife Sita, after his conquest of Ravana, who had kidnapped her.

In Northern India, Divali marks the beginning of the Hindu New Year, and many families celebrate with rituals to honour Lakshmi, their goddess of prosperity and wealth. In Gujarat and Malaysia it is the practice to clean and paint the home and to draw *alpanas*, or elaborate designs, on their floors with coloured rice flour to welcome Lakshmi. Divas are placed everywhere—in courtyards, window ledges, roofs, fences or doorways—because it is believed that Lakshmi will not bless a home that has not been illuminated to greet her.

Jainists commemorate the death of their hero Mahavira in the city of Pava, and this day is called *Dipavali*, *Deva Dewali*, or *Mahavir Nirvana*.

In Nepal, the New Year and Lakshmi are celebrated on *Tihar*.

In northern India, many young girls place their divas on small rafts and set them afloat on a river. If the lamp stays alight until it has floated out of sight or reached the other side its owner will have good fortune for the year.

The Divali festival is as important to Hindus as Christmas is to Christians, and it is celebrated with the same joyous enthusiasm. The five hundred million Hindus around the world visit with friends and relatives to exchange gifts and cards, and there is feasting (meals are typically vegetarian) and prayers in the temples. In the evenings there are dramatic fireworks displays filling the skies with blazing colours.

Here in Canada Divali is usually a one-day celebration, with lights, greetings, entertainment and worship. Although the diva lamps are only lit inside homes or temples, some stores choose to decorate with multicoloured strings of lights.

Children may enjoy making a diva lamp to celebrate and it is quite a simple process. Roll out a piece of clay to a thickness of about five millimetres. Cut two ovals from the clay, one slightly larger than the other. (Some people draw their ovals first on paper, cut them out and then trace them onto the clay). Scratch the centres of both ovals to make two rough surfaces. Join the rough surfaces together using a little slurry (clay mixed with water to make it slightly runny). The small oval should lie on top of the larger one. Carefully turn up the edges of the smaller oval and make a lip at one end. Turn up the edges of the larger oval all the way around. Fire the lamp by baking it on a cookie sheet in the oven. You may paint the diva when it has baked and cooled. Place a short piece of candle inside and light it.

Our American neighbours and Americans living in Canada celebrate Thanksgiving on the third Thursday of this month. An interesting historical note shows that of the one hundred and two pilgrims who set forth on the Mayflower, only fifty-one sat down to the first Thanksgiving dinner in 1621. The other half of the group lay buried on a nearby hill, victims of disease and privation.

Today, Thanksgiving is a time for family reunions and traditions, the most popular, of course, being the elaborate dinner featuring turkey and its many accompaniments.

Come ye, thankful people, come,
Raise the song of harvest home!
All is safely gathered in,
'Ere the winter storms begin;
God, our maker doth provide
For our wants to be supplied;
Come to God's own temple, come,
Raise the song of harvest home!

Dear Alfred: The Hymnal

November is the month when we are able to visit the Royal Agricultural Winter Fair. "The Royal," as it is known, is a unique opportunity to experience the richness of our agricultural heritage and the excellence of the agriculture and food industry that has made Canada a world leader.

Held at the Coliseum at Exhibition Place in Toronto, the Royal is the world's largest indoor agricultural fair and international equestrian competition.

I have enjoyed the Royal Winter Fair for years and I recommend it highly for all ages!

November 11th is the feast day of St. Martin of Tours. One of the most popular saints of the Middle Ages, he was known for his kindness and generosity. One legend recounts the story of St. Martin meeting a beggar. Having no money to give, St. Martin split his cloak in two with his sword and gave half to the shivering man.

This feast is also known as Martinmas in many countries of Europe. Because this day comes after the harvest, when the new wine is ready, St. Martin is considered to be the patron of wine growers and tavern keepers.

Thanks for the harvest is also observed with a feast where goose is the traditional meal. Swedes know this day as Martin's Goose Day and some Swedish-Canadians still have a Goose Fest on November 11th.

St. Catherine is another popular saint whose feast day is celebrated in November. Sentenced to death by Emperor Maxentius for her extraordinary success in converting people to Christianity, it is said that she was tortured on a spiked wheel. Although she was saved by divine intervention, the Emperor then had her beheaded. Today, there is a firework that spins in pinwheel style throwing off multicoloured lights. It is known as a Catherine Wheel. Gymnasts who perform cartwheels are thought to be repeating the motion of St. Catherine on the dreadful wheel of torture.

In Canada, *la Sainte-Catherine*, celebrated by French Canadians on November 25th, has its own special custom. A beloved seventeenth-century teacher, Marguerite Bourgeoys, had her students make *la tire de la Ste. Catherine* (St. Catherine's taffy) as a way to encourage children to attend school.

My good friend Hélène Ellison, a native of Montreal, gave me her recipe for *la tire*, and it is quite delicious. Hélène tells me that the secret to perfect taffy is the use of a candy thermometer. Although it is possible to make it without a thermometer, it is a bit more of a risk.

Saint Catherine's Pull Taffy

1 cup molasses
1 cup white sugar
1 cup brown sugar

1 cup corn syrup

1 tbsp. vinegar

1 tbsp. butter

1 tsp. baking soda

1/2 cup water

1. Grease well a cookie sheet that has an edge.
2. In a pot, mix together all of the ingredients except the baking soda.
3. Bring to a boil and continue to boil until a teaspoonful of the liquid forms a hard ball when dropped into cold water, or until a candy thermometer reads 240° F or 115° C.
4. Add the baking soda and stir until mixed well.
5. Pour onto the greased cookie sheet.
6. Allow to cool. When the taffy is cool enough to pick up, smear your hands with butter and pull until taffy is golden. Cut taffy into bite-size pieces.

The last day of November is also a special feast day. Scottish, Polish and Persian-Canadians celebrate St. Andrew's Day on November 30th.

One of Christ's twelve apostles, Andrew was a disciple of John the Baptist, and the brother of Peter. St. Andrew's association with Scotland came about four centuries after his death, when some of his relics were brought to Scotland. Some Scots also believe that his body was buried on the coast of Fife.

Scottish-Canadians enjoy a dinner on the Saturday closest to November 30th. This dinner is much in the manner of a Robbie Burns Day feast, including haggis and "singed sheep's head." Russians, who say that St. Andrew preached in Moscow in the first century, join the Scots in laying claim to St. Andrew as their patron saint.

Polish girls have a unique tradition for St. Andrew's Day. *Andrzyki* (or "Andrew's games") is a kind of fortune-telling that predicts coming romance. The girls break off dry branches from cherry trees, plant them in wet sand and then tend them with great care. It is said that if a girl's branch blooms by Christmas, she will marry within the year.

The flag of St. Andrew, a white diagonal cross on a blue background, is a part of the Union Jack.

December

Sometime last night snow began to fall,
So gently did it come, so softly white;
Its music we failed to hear at all
As it whispered to the listening night.

It is pure and beautiful outside—
Within, my room is cozy warm.
A sense of peace within me abides
As I look out at the first snowstorm.

Growing up, as I did, on Canada's East Coast, the weather during Advent was often considered to be a harbinger of the winter to come. It was an old Acadian belief that a cold, miserable Advent meant that we would have a mild winter. If Advent weather was more temperate, it was almost sure to be a long, harsh winter.

The fourth Sunday before Christmas marks the beginning of Advent and, for many families, this is the start of the Christmas season. In our home, the Sunday before Advent was also a special occasion. It was known as "stir-up Sunday," an old Anglican tradition that came from a prayer on the last Sunday of the Church's year:

Stir up, we beseech thee, O Lord, the wills of thy faithful people, that they plenteously bring forth the fruit of good works, may of thee be plenteously rewarded; through Jesus Christ our Lord.

In the kitchen, we had to stir up the mincemeat and the Christmas pudding and cake. Each person who came to our home stirred the pot three times in the name of the Father, Son and Holy Ghost.

Advent has its own special traditions. The Advent wreath, a circle of greenery in which four candles are set, originated with the German Lutherans. One candle is lit the first Sunday, two are lit the second Sunday and so on until the fourth Sunday. A large white candle in the centre of the wreath is lit on Christmas Day.

The Advent calendar also originated in Germany. These are elaborate calendars with twenty-four windows used to count down the days until Christmas. Some calendars have pictures behind the windows, but the more popular Canadian calendars have a piece of chocolate as a treat for the youngsters who anxiously await the arrival of Christmas Day.

In the past, Advent was a period of fasting, when no meat, cheese or alcoholic drinks could be consumed. This is no longer true, although some do choose to fast at this time.

December 6th is the day for Finnish-Canadians to celebrate the independence of their country of origin. On this date in 1917, Finland broke free from Russian control and declared its independence. Wherever there are sizable numbers of Finns across Canada, the Finnish community sponsors Independence Day programs, and commemorative services are held in the churches.

While my great-grandchildren will anxiously await the arrival of Santa Claus on Christmas Eve, many youngsters who are of Dutch or German origin will be expecting St. Nicholas, or Sinterklaas, on the night of December 5th. This is the eve of St. Nicholas Day, December 6th, and is one of the oldest and most popular of all Dutch traditions.

Very little is known about St. Nicholas, but, according to legend, he was born in Lycia, Asia Minor, and, in the early fourth century, he was the Bishop of Myra in what is now known as Turkey. Known for his kindness and charitable deeds, particularly to children, it is said that he provided bags of gold for three young girls, giving each a dowry and saving them from a life of prostitution. This is possibly the source of St. Nicholas' association with gift giving.

In the Netherlands, on December 6th, St. Nicholas still rides into town on a white horse wearing his red mitre. *Zwarte Piet*, or Black Peter, a companion or helper who is dressed in the Moorish costume of a page, precedes him. Black Peter carries St. Nicholas' bag, which contains candy and gifts for the good children and a switch in order to punish those children who have been bad.

German children leave their shoes outside their bedroom doors on the eve of December 6th, believing that St. Nicholas will leave them small gifts if they have been good.

Dutch children leave out hay and carrots for the Saint's horse, much as my great-grandchildren leave carrots and apples for Santa's reindeer.

Gifts for the children are not wrapped in paper but are placed in whatever ingenious containers that their parents can find. It is not unusual for a gift to be placed in a hollowed-out cabbage, for example. Each gift also contains a humourous poem that usually connects the gift and the container to the person. For example, a gift hidden inside a child's plastic telephone may remind a young teen that they talk too much on the phone.

In Canada, Dutch parents relate the traditional folk tales of *Sinterklaas* and *Zwarte Piet* on the eve of St. Nicholas Day. It is a special family time of gift-giving and enjoying traditional Dutch foods.

For German and other European-Canadian children, it is also a time to exchange gifts and enjoy family gatherings and delicious dinners together.

Many Japanese Buddhists celebrate December 8th as the anniversary of Buddha's enlightenment, or *Bodhi*. It is said that Buddha sat for forty-nine days under the Bodhi tree to find the answer to the riddle of life.

On December 8th there is another celebration for the Japanese. In a ceremony dating back to the fourth century A.D., a requiem service is held for sewing needles. Called *Hari Kuyo*, the Festival of Broken Needles, the services are attended by tailors, dressmakers and even those who sew at home. Set up in the style of the traditional Shinto shrine, a sacred rope with white paper stripes is suspended over the three-tiered altar. On the top tier are offerings of cake and fruits. The second tier holds a pan of tofu and the third and lowest tier offers a place to put scissors and thimbles.

I find the tofu to be a very interesting part of the ceremony. This is where people insert their broken or bent needles while offering prayers of thanks for the needles' years of service. *Sutras* are also recited for the repose of the needles. After the service, the needles are wrapped in paper and laid to rest in the sea.

Although it is not a common tradition here, some Japanese-Canadians in the west hold a *Hari Kuyo* on this date.

One of the loveliest observances at this time of year is St. Lucia Day, or, as Swedes call it, *Luciadagen*. This festival of light, which marks the beginning of the Christmas season for people of the Scandinavian countries of Denmark, Norway and Sweden, is held on

December 13th, although the original St. Lucia Day used to fall on the solstice.

Legend has it that St. Lucia was betrothed, against her will, to a pagan nobleman. He claimed that her beautiful eyes haunted him day and night. In an attempt to end the engagement, she supposedly cut out her eyes and sent them to her suitor. God rewarded her sacrifice by giving her even more beautiful eyes. For this she is known as patron saint of the blind.

"Lucia" means light, and all of the traditional ceremonies for the day centre on a beautiful St. Lucia, dressed in a shining white robe, and lighting the darkness with a crown of candles.

It is traditional to dress the oldest daughter in a family in a white robe tied with a crimson sash. The metal crown, covered with lingonberry leaves, with its burning white candles, is placed on her head. Younger girls, also dressed in white, are given tinsel halos, while boys wear white robes and cone-shaped hats of silver paper, and carry star-topped sceptres. On the morning of the 13th, they awaken the family members by delivering a tray of saffron buns or ginger cookies and coffee to their bed.

Some years ago, George and the girls and I visited Scandinavian friends in Nova Scotia. That year, their daughter, Margit, was selected as the "Lucia Bride" and crowned with a magnificent golden crown that was handcrafted in Sweden. We joined the many celebrants at a smorgasbord dinner known as the Julbord Feast, and after dinner there was a delightful presentation of Swedish Christmas songs, folk dances and a Lucia procession. Margit, with her crown of burning candles, led the other children, who each carried a single candle. It was a beautiful sight in the early winter darkness.

A "Queen of Light" presides over the festivities in Ontario, and in the Prairie Provinces, where there are large numbers of Scandinavian-Canadians, similar celebrations and pageants are organized.

Canadians hailing from the Caribbean island of St. Lucia hold a "Feast for St. Lucy" in Toronto. This is often a dinner-dance honouring the saint who is a symbol of the preciousness of light and patron saint of the Caribbean island, which is named for her.

Mexican-Canadians have a most interesting way to prepare for Christmas. A nine-day celebration, from December 16 to 24, commemorates the journey of Mary and Joseph from Nazareth to Bethlehem, and their search for shelter. These processions, or *losadas*, take place each night for nine nights as a couple, dressed as Joseph and Mary, go from home to home seeking shelter. As it was in Bethlehem, the couple are turned away until they knock on the door of the home that has been chosen to host the party that evening. With their arrival, the *posada* (party) begins. The highlight of each party is the breaking of the *piñata*. The children are blindfolded and given a chance to swing a stick at the *piñata,* a papier-mâché animal, hanging by a string from the ceiling and filled with toys and candies).

The *posatas* are repeated for nine evenings, the last being Christmas Eve. That evening, known as *Noche Buena*, or the Good Night, the pilgrimage ends when the procession arrives at the church for midnight Mass. This Mass is known as the *Misa de Gallo*, or Mass of the Cock because it is held so early, ending just after midnight.

December 21 or 22 is the winter solstice. The shortest day of the year in the Northern Hemisphere, it is also the first day of winter. In areas of the Far North there will be no daylight hours at all today! There were many pre-Christian traditions marking winter solstice, and bonfires were often a part of these rites.

Some traditional Chinese families in Canada may observe the Chinese Festival of the Winter Solstice with services of prayers to their ancestors. The Chinese have great respect for parents and ancestors and many of their festivals honour the older generation, both living and dead.

Hanukkah is a Jewish celebration that takes place around the time of the winter solstice and lasts for eight days. Hanukkah celebrates religious freedom and commemorates the successful rebellion of the Jews against the Syrians in the Maccabean War of 162 B.C.

After the victory the Temple was cleansed and purified and rededicated, and the Menorah, or perpetual lamp, was re-lit. As the story goes there was only one jar of sacred oil left but by some miracle this one jar kept the holy lamp burning for eight days.

Jewish families today celebrate the miracle by lighting a special candelabrum known as a *chanukkiyah*. One brightly coloured candle is lit each night until all eight candles are lit—always using the *shammus*, or helper candle, to light the candles in the Menorah. A special prayer is recited during the lighting of the candles, and while the candles burn it is a time for songs and games and the giving of gifts to the children.

One of the most popular games is the dreidel game, played with a four-sided top. On each of the four sides of the dreidel there is one Hebrew letter—*Nu, Shin, Gimmel and Heh*—representing the words *"new gadol hayeh sham"* or "a great miracle happened there."

Children often play the dreidel game with Hanukkah *gelt*, or coins made of chocolate and wrapped in gold foil. Each child places a set number of coins in a common pot. They then, in turn, spin the dreidel and when the top stops the letter that is upright determines the outcome. "Nu" means nothing is added to the pot; "Shin" means one coin must be added to the pot; "Gimmel" means the player may take all of the coins in the pot; and "Heh" means a player may take half of the coins in the pot. (If a player lands on *Gimmel* and takes all of the coins each of the players must ante in two coins for the game to continue.) The game ends when each player has spun a predetermined number of spins or a time limit has been reached.

The *latke*, a potato pancake, is one food that is traditionally served at Hannukah celebrations. My dear friend Ester Schwartz sent me her recipe for latkes and our family loves them served with sour cream and applesauce.

Latkes

2 cups coarsely grated potatoes (uncooked)

2 eggs, separated

1 tsp. salt

1 rounded tbsp. flour or matzo meal

1 onion, grated

1. Combine potatoes, egg yolks, salt, flour and onion.
2. Beat egg whites and fold into the mixture. Drop by the spoonful in a skillet with 1/2 inch of sizzling oil. Fry latkes on both sides until golden brown.
3. Drain on paper towels and serve hot with sour cream and/or apple sauce.

Our Anglican church calendar used to name the day of the solstice, December 21st, St. Thomas Day. You may remember that St. Thomas the Apostle was named "Doubting Thomas" because after the Resurrection, when the other Apostles told Thomas that they had seen Jesus, he refused to believe them until he had touched Jesus' wounds himself.

At one time it was the practice for widows or poor women to go door-to-door collecting gifts of food, clothing or money to help them through the long winter. This was called "going a-Thomasing" and many families might never have survived had it not been for the generosity of the neighbours on St. Thomas Day.

'Twas the night before Christmas
And all through the house,
Not a creature was stirring
Not even a mouse.

The now-immortal poem "A Visit from St. Nicholas" was written by Clement Moore for his children back in 1822. My grandson Marshall laughed with me the other day as he remarked, "You know that this poem was written a very long time ago, Gran. 'The night before Christmas . . . not a creature was stirring' meant that they weren't frantically trying to put together some complicated child's toy in order that it be in working condition by Christmas morning. Last year I was trying to assemble a wagon for Michael—

a degree in engineering would have been an asset! It also didn't help that the only set of instructions was in Japanese and I couldn't make any sense of the drawings."

Here in Canada Christmas Eve is celebrated in many different ways, and each family has its own traditions.

For French-Canadian families it is the custom for all of the family to come together for Christmas Eve. The midnight Mass, or *minuette*, is celebrated, after which the family returns home for the *reveillon*, a wonderful dinner for family and friends. Gifts are opened after Mass and children may stay up as late as they wish. In the Pouliot home in Quebec City, every one of the five children always tried to stay awake all night, but by 1:30 or 2 a.m. all eyes were closed and the children would be sleeping soundly. *Tourtière* and soup with hot home-made bread is always a delicious part of *le reveillon* at the Pouliot home.

The midnight church service celebrating the birth of Jesus is the main Christmas Eve tradition for Christians of all denominations. Many European-Canadians eat a large but meatless meal before attending church, because it is a fast day.

Polish-Canadians celebrate this night much as the Ukrainian Canadians do on January 6th (Christmas Eve on the Julian calendar). Celebrations begin when the first star is seen, and that star symbolizes the Star of Bethlehem. The Polish *Wigilia* is the most solemn event of the year and is celebrated with the most beautiful tablecloth and the finest cutlery and china on which to serve a twelve-course meatless dinner. One extra place is always set for any stranger who may arrive, and also in memory of relatives who have passed away during the year.

After Mass, when the fast has ended, Poles enjoy a hunter's stew of cabbage, sauerkraut, onions, mushrooms, *kielbasa* sausage, beef ribs and other meats.

Carolling, going from house to house singing Christmas Carols, is also a Christmas Eve tradition in many areas. This tradition began in the Middle Ages and came to North America with the English settlers.

Italian-Canadians also get together in family groups on Christmas Eve. After a meatless meal the family will head off to the church. An impressive part of the Italian celebration is the *presepio*, or the crèche, a model of the Nativity scene. It is not unusual to have life-size figures of Mary, Joseph, and baby Jesus in the manger and worshipping angels, shepherds and animals both inside and outside the church. It is said that St. Francis of Assisi actually used live animals and people in his *presepio*.

In Newfoundland and Nova Scotia, mummers or *belsnickers* go from house to house on Christmas Eve. These people are groups of rowdy carollers who are in masks or costumes. They sing or dance, play instruments and generally act up until the neighbours guess who they are. At that time the costumes come off and they become normal visitors.

In our family it is our custom to enjoy a light supper, usually soup and sandwiches, before heading off to church to watch the children's presentation of the Christmas story. All of my children, grandchildren and great-grandchildren have been involved in the Christmas pageant at one time or another.

I believe the finest performance by a McCann family member was given by my daughter Julia many years ago. Although she was only about five or six years old she was a very self-confident little girl and was selected to be Mary for the Christmas pageant. All was well until Mary and Joseph arrived at the "inn" and Joseph asked for a room. When the innkeeper announced that "There is no room at the inn," Mary/Julia walked over to the innkeeper and in her most determined voice said "My husband said we're tired and we . . . want . . . a . . . room!" With that, Julia gave the innkeeper one almighty poke in the arm. The innkeeper, a rather whiny seven-year-old, started to cry and look for his mother.

"Ha!" said Julia "Come on Joseph. Let's get a good place to stay here."

Joseph, not knowing what else to do, followed Julia to the crèche scene near the altar.

The audience, by now, was nearly on the floor.

Julia was not asked to be Mary again.

After church we usually head home to bed so that we may enjoy Christmas day to the fullest.

Unto us a child is born, unto us a son is given.

Isaiah 9:6

Christmas, the celebration of the birth of Jesus, is observed by Christians around the world. As a holiday, Christmas is a strange joining of Christian and pagan traditions. Decorating with holly, ivy and mistletoe, indulging in eating and drinking, exchanging gifts and stringing lights on trees can all be traced back to *Saturnalia*, or the rites of winter solstice. The Yule log, which burned during the Christmas season, was probably part of the winter solstice rite of burning bonfires to celebrate the return of longer days.

Today, the *Buche de Noël*, or Yule Log, is a chocolate cake with white icing "snow" that symbolizes the Yule log of years gone by.

The custom of decorating evergreen trees is borrowed from Germany. Martin Luther is said to have had the idea when he saw the stars twinkling over the evergreen trees while he was walking. The lights on the tree would be symbolic of the heavens from where Christ came. Although candles provided the early lights, most trees are now decorated with strings of electric lights. Many cities across the country decorate an enormous evergreen tree, often at City Hall. *Kado Matsu* is an old Japanese tradition that sees families go into the woods to cut down a pine tree to place near their front door in the week before New Year's Day. The evergreen is a symbol of strength and long life.

Christmas day is most often a time of family get-togethers and wonderful traditional Christmas dinners. Of course, your tradition depends on your roots. In our family we enjoy a turkey dinner with mashed potatoes and gravy. Across our country the traditional meal may include reindeer, roast goose, *tamales*, gingerbread, *stollen* or *torrone*. Whatever you choose to eat, I hope you will enjoy it in the company of family and good friends.

Boxing Day on the 26th gets its name from the English custom of giving Christmas boxes of food and money to family servants, tradespeople and others. The boxes were usually little earthenware boxes that were carried from house to house to collect tips and year-end bonuses. For centuries December 26th was also known as St. Stephen's Day.

December 26th is the day that *Kwanzaa*, a relatively new celebration, begins. A cultural festival, Kwanzaa was founded in 1966 by Dr. Maulana

Karenga, a college professor in California, to encourage people of African origin to celebrate their rich heritage.

Kwanzaa is a Kiswahili word meaning "the first fruits of the harvest." The festival is based on seven principles. One of the seven is highlighted each day of the holiday. A seven-branched candelabrum holds three green candles to symbolize hopes for the future and one black candle, in the centre, to represent the African-American people.

Families gather each evening to light a candle and to discuss the principle of the day. On the evening of the 31st there is a community feast or *karamu*.

In Canada, Kwanzaa customs are still developing but it is becoming more important and more widely celebrated each year.

December 31st, the last day of the year, is celebrated in many ways. For some it is a time to attend midnight church services. For others it is a time to gather in a public place and count down the final seconds of the old year.

Our family has a tradition that has developed over the years. We like to take down the calendar on which we kept track of family events, and reread the events of each month. It is a kind of walk down memory lane that reminds us of the good times (and bad), the joys and the sorrows that make up life in each year.

It may not sound like a very exciting New Year's Eve celebration but you'd be surprised how enjoyable it really is.

In this book I have tried to give an overview of some of the customs and traditions that we in Canada celebrate each year. Although I have done my best to be as accurate as possible, I hope that you will understand if some small errors have crept into my work.

I would like to think that tolerance is also a part of the heritage that we enjoy in this great country. Hopefully, gaining a greater knowledge of the many exciting and varied cultures in Canada will also help to increase the tolerance and respect we must show one another.